Insights from Film into Violence and Oppression

Shattered Dreams of the Good Life

Edited by John P. Lovell

Westport, Connecticut
London

Library of Congress Cataloging-in-Publication Data

Insights from film into violence and oppression : shattered dreams
  of the good life / edited by John P. Lovell.
     p.   cm.
  Filmography: p.
  Includes bibliographical references and index.
  ISBN 0–275–95972–4 (alk. paper)
  1. Violence in motion pictures.   2. Social problems in motion
pictures.   I. Lovell, John P., 1932–
PN1995.9.V5V56   1998
791.43′655—dc21   97–23878

British Library Cataloguing in Publication Data is available.

Library of Congress Catalog Card Number: 97–23878
ISBN: 0–275–95972–4

First published in 1998

Praeger Publishers, 88 Post Road West, Westport, CT 06881
An imprint of Greenwood Publishing Group, Inc.

Printed in the United States of America

The paper used in this book complies with the
Permanent Paper Standard issued by the National
Information Standards Organization (Z39.48–1984).

10 9 8 7 6 5 4 3 2 1

To Charlene Brown

Contents

Preface   ix

Part I: Issues

1. **Structural Violence, Peace, and the Good Life**
   William J. Meyer   3

2. **She Doth Protest Too Much, or Does She?**
   An Essay on Gender, Violence, and Domination
   Jean C. Robinson   23

3. **Exploring Sexual and Political Domination**
   through Film
   Barbara Allen   39

4. **Shattered but Not Broken: Images of Structural**
   Violence and War by Black Women Filmmakers
   Gloria J. Gibson   67

5. **Bugles, Bandoliers, and Body Bags: The Soldier's**
   Saga through Film
   John P. Lovell   83

Part II: Caveats

6. **Making the Classroom a Safe Environment**
   Barbara Allen   105

7. **Why Did the Chicken Cross the Screen?**
   Cognitive and Emotional Considerations in
   Using Film to Teach about the Manhattan Project
   and Hiroshima
   David Pace   113

Part III: Resources

8. **Sample Study and Discussion Guides**
   John P. Lovell with contributions from William
   Meyer, Jean Robinson, Barbara Allen and
   Gloria Gibson   129

9. **A Bibliographic Essay on Using Film to Teach**
   about Peace Studies and Structural Violence
   Kristine R. Brancolini   141

10. **Filmography**
    Kristine R. Brancolini   161

Index   165

About the Contributors   171

Preface

This is a book about the shattering of dreams. One can find evidence in virtually every society of the modern world of dreams of the "good life." The specific elements that constitute "the good life" vary enormously, of course, not only across cultures but also across subcultures. Moreover, if a privileged few sometimes are able over a period of years to sustain the pursuit of their dreams, for most people harsh realities intrude. The latter experience tends to be the characteristic fate of oppressed segments of society, the focus of this book. More precisely, the focus is on the violence, from domestic and international sources, to which the socially downtrodden are especially vulnerable. It is not only physical violence that can transform dreams into nightmares but also "structural violence," or institutionalized social structures and patterns of discrimination that thwart human potential.

Motion pictures and videos, as the various chapters in this volume reveal, have the potential for bringing to life otherwise abstract concepts that teachers find important in explaining social phenomena. Through film, the student is able vicariously to share experiences he or she might otherwise find remote and therefore puzzling. As authors of the chapters that follow make clear, the pedagogical value of a skillfully crafted film lies not only in its portrayal of injustice through the experiences of individuals with which students can identify, but also in its capacity to provide some vivid and memorable lessons in strength of character, courage, and acts of selflessness in the face of adversity.

Domestic and international violence are objects of concern in numerous college and university courses in the social sciences and humanities; in various multidisciplinary programs such as women's studies, Afro-American studies, and Hispanic studies; and in some professional schools such as law, journalism, and education. Film, properly utilized, can be a powerful medium for helping students gain an understanding of the roots and consequences of domestic and international violence. Various specialized texts on film are available that are suitable for film studies courses. However, to the best of our knowledge, there is no book currently available that meets the needs of the classroom teacher whose interest is not film study per se but rather the use of film as a pedagogical tool.

This book has the distinctive merit of incorporating a discussion of film into an examination of issues related to violence, informed by the in-depth knowledge that the authors bring to their subjects from a variety of disciplinary and interdisciplinary perspectives and their familiarity with the needs of classroom teachers in various disciplines.

During 1989–90, its first year of operation, the Indiana Center on Global Change and World Peace (ICGCWP) collaborated with the IU Honors Division in conducting a faculty/student retreat devoted to the examination of violence as a recurring theme in contemporary international politics. With special reference to the American experience, participants were asked to consider the implications of a drastically altered global milieu in which the traditional enemy, the Soviet Union, no longer exists. Notre Dame Professor George Lopez presented an afternoon guest lecture on "The Changing Nature of Violence around the Globe." That evening, participants watched and discussed a provocative documentary film, *Faces of the Enemy*. The following morning was devoted to an in-depth and far-reaching continuing discussion, guided by Professor Lopez, of issues raised in or suggested by the lecture and the film.

The success of this retreat in stimulating an active exchange of ideas about issues of violence prompted the ICGCWP and the Honors Division, joined by the Black Film Archive and the Women's Study Program, to organize a workshop in February 1991 and another a year later using film as the medium to stimulate discussion of issues of violence. (The specific workshop theme changed somewhat from one year to the next; but violence in domestic context and in an international context was of central concern in each workshop.)

Each of the workshops included several films, U.S.-produced and foreign, with the entire film or a long excerpt shown to all 36 workshop participants (twelve-each faculty members, graduate students, and undergraduate honors students, with men and women represented equally). After each film showing, participants were organized into small groups (typically six per group—two-each undergrad, grad student, and faculty) for sustained discussion. The various small groups shared their conclusions with one another at a plenary session at the end of the workshop.

A similar film workshop was conducted in 1992, with gratifying results. Again, student and faculty participants found the experience to be thought provoking and extremely helpful in sorting out their ideas about violence. Faculty members and graduate students also took from the workshop a number of ideas for application in their own teaching.

This book has benefited from the discussions in the various film workshops and the classes in which the films discussed herein were shown. Although it is not feasible to name all the faculty and students who participated, they have our gratitude. Our thanks extend also to Charlene Brown and her staff, Pat Haney, Dan Sisken, Sander Valyocsik, Sami Barudi, Patrick O'Meara, Judith Rice, and Kim Foust for their invaluable assistance.

Part I

Issues

—————— 1 ——————

Structural Violence, Peace, and the Good Life

William J. Meyer

As hopes of a "new world order" fade into the savage ethnic conflicts of the 1990s, students of human society are challenged to look anew at our understandings of peace, violence, and community. Are the underlying sources of human conflict economic at root, as many have long and commonly assumed, or are they, in some or many cases, cultural? In other words, would human conflict and violence be eliminated if we achieved a fair and just distribution of land, jobs, income, and educational opportunities for all members of society, or do the sources of conflict go beyond a full belly, a decent wage, and a roof over our head? For example, are people killing each other in the former Yugoslavia because they feel economically deprived relative to other ethnic groups or because they have concluded that they can no longer successfully pursue or achieve the "good life" in a pluralistic, multireligious society? The answers to these timely questions are informed by and related to our definitions and understandings of violence, peace, and the good life.

In this chapter, I shall examine issues of violence, peace, and the good life in relation to three American films: *The Grapes of Wrath*, *Do the Right Thing*, and *A Raisin in the Sun*. My aim is twofold: first, to set forth, explain, and interpret some key concepts that can help us better understand the relationships among violence, peace, and the good life; and second, to apply these concepts to the films as a way to illuminate important issues and raise thoughtful and provocative questions. Hence, I shall divide the essay into two parts. Part one will set forth some theoretical and interpretive "tools" and part two will use those tools to analyze and illuminate key issues raised by the films. More specifically, I shall examine, in part one, the notion of "structural violence" and its conception of peace and then show how it ties into one of the central debates in contemporary political theory, namely, the debate between "liberals" and "communitarians." Though these terms are often bandied about by politicians, this debate among political philosophers focuses on the important question of how best to organize human society. Is society best organized around a common and shared conception of the good life, as communitarians contend, or is society best organized when it secures the means and freedom for each individual to pursue his or her own conception of the good life, as liberals maintain? I then go on to examine a specific conception of the good life proposed by the philosopher Mortimer Adler. After discussing these concepts and debates, I turn my attention, in part two, to the three films. The first film, *The Grapes of Wrath*, based on John Steinbeck's famous novel, vividly portrays economic and class forms of structural violence. The second film, Spike Lee's *Do the Right Thing*, goes beyond economic and class issues to look at ethnic and race relations in the context of a New York neighborhood. Finally, the third film, *A Raisin in the Sun*, based on the play by Lorraine Hansberry, deals with the conflicts and hopes of a black family in Chicago as it seeks the good life in a society dominated by whites. To be sure, my analysis of these films will not be exhaustive but, rather, simply illustrative of the issues and questions at hand.[1]

SOME THEORETICAL AND INTERPRETIVE "TOOLS"

The concept of "structural violence" is most closely identified with the work of the Scandinavian scholar Johan Galtung. Galtung recognizes that the concept of violence is inescapably tied to its inverse notion of peace, like two sides of the same coin. Thus, in order to define violence, Galtung begins by defining peace. As a starting point, he offers three principles:

1. The term "peace" shall be used for social goals at least verbally agreed to by many, if not necessarily by most.

2. These social goals may be difficult, but not impossible, to attain.

3. The statement "peace is absence of violence" shall be retained as valid.[2]

As evidenced by this third principle, Galtung is willing to accept and affirm the standard definition of peace as being the "absence of violence." In doing so, he has two aims in mind. First, he accepts the premise that, whatever peace is, it certainly must be characterized by the absence of physical violence. War zones cannot be defined as conditions of peace in anyone's lexicon. Galtung's second aim is to direct renewed attention to the definition of violence. If peace is indeed the absence of violence, then, as Galtung puts it, "everything now hinges on making a definition of 'violence.' . . . [For] if peace action is to be regarded highly because it is action against violence, then the concept of violence must be broad enough to include the most significant varieties, yet specific enough to serve as a basis for concrete action."3 As this passage suggests, Galtung's primary concern is to make sure that the concept of violence is broad enough to encompass its "most significant varieties" and to include its most invidious manifestations. In short, Galtung aims at a comprehensive definition of violence.

His definition reads as follows: "*violence is present when human beings are being influenced so that their actual somatic and mental realizations are below their potential realizations.*"4 The crux of this definition lies in the distinction between "actual realizations" and "potential realizations." What Galtung is claiming is that human beings suffer violence whenever they are influenced in such a way that their actual achievements and realizations in life fall below what they could potentially achieve, given the current level of insights and resources available at any particular time. In other words, violence is "the cause of the difference between the potential and the actual, between what could have been and what is."5 Galtung offers two examples to illustrate his point.

If, for instance, a person died of tuberculosis in the eighteenth century, when no medical treatment or cure was available, then that would not be an example of violence because the necessary insights to treat tuberculosis had not yet been discovered. However, if a person died today of the same disease, given the presence of an abundant level of resources, knowledge, and technology, then violence is present as it was possible to prevent the death. In other words, to die of tuberculosis today is due to a lack of distribution of adequate health care rather than to a lack of medical know-how. Alternatively, if a person today dies in an earthquake, because adequate detection and prevention skills and technology are still not yet fully developed, this is not an instance of violence. However, if and when in the future such predictive capabilities do exist, then death due to earthquakes will also be an instance of violence.6

What is interesting to note here is that when someone dies in an earthquake, we often say that they died "a violent death." Yet, according to Galtung's definition, no violence has occurred in a strict sense. What both of these illustrations reveal is that Galtung links violence ultimately to human culpability and guilt. Violence occurs only when human action, either individual or collective, could have and should have acted in some manner to prevent the discrepancy between actual and potential realizations from occurring. In many cases, this collective violence is insidiously embedded in the social and economic structures of society, which is precisely why Galtung and others call it "structural" violence. Because the violence is embedded in social structures and, thus, hidden from plain view, the violence and its corresponding culpability are usually overlooked. For instance, in the case of someone dying of tuberculosis today, it would seem, from outward appearances, that no violence has occurred because the person died of a disease. But Galtung would argue that no person need die of tuberculosis today, given our present level of medical knowledge; thus, the root cause of this person's death is a neglect of adequate distribution of health care. Galtung's main concern is not to point fingers of guilt but, rather, to draw our attention to the many forms of violence that occur everyday that are so embedded in the "way things are" that we completely overlook them. His goal is to change fundamental aspects of social, political, and economic structures in order to lessen and, ultimately, eliminate the various forms of structural violence.

To return to Galtung's two illustrations: both of them deal with actualizations and potentialities of "somatic" or bodily goods, for example, the enjoyment of physical health free from illness (tuberculosis) and free from injury or death (earthquake). But Galtung admits, and this is what I want to develop, that the issue becomes much more ambiguous when one begins to speak of "mental" potential realizations. The concept of "potential realizations," either somatic or mental, is always evaluative or normative in character. That is to say, it entails some assessment and implicit claim about the good life—some claim about what is good for human beings as such and, thus, what potential humans ought to realize in order to live happy, fulfilling lives. Galtung suggests that it is generally easier for persons to agree about "somatic" goods than "mental" goods. For instance, almost everyone agrees that bodily health, nutritious food, and adequate shelter are necessary components of a good life. Yet, when one turns to "mental" goods, the ability to reach consensus becomes much more difficult. More precisely, it becomes more difficult to achieve consensus on certain types of mental goods.

Galtung makes an implicit distinction between two main types of mental goods. The first type I shall call "mental capacities," such as the capacity to read, to write, to think, and to communicate. The second type is what I call "value orientations." By "value orientations" I mean those underlying religious and/or philosophical views of life by which individuals and communities identify sources of value and interpret the meaning of existence. Galtung believes there is a consensus on the importance of possessing certain mental capacities but there remains much disagreement about questions of value orientations. He offers a vivid illustration of this distinction, which is quite revealing of his overall position. "Literacy is held in high regard almost everywhere, whereas the value of being Christian is highly controversial. Hence, we would talk about violence if the level of literacy is lower than what it could have been, not if the level of Christianity is lower than what it could have been."[7]

In this passage, Galtung attaches different normative weight or significance to these two kinds of mental goods (literacy and Christianity) based on whether there is actual widespread consensus regarding their value or importance. It is essential to recall here that Galtung's first principle defines peace (and, in turn, violence) in terms of "social goals at least verbally agreed to by many, if not necessarily by most." In other words, he claims that violence occurs only in those cases where there is widespread agreement about the desirability or importance of a particular social good. Thus, in our present example, he says that literacy is highly regarded almost everywhere, whereas the importance or value of being Christian "is highly controversial." In light of this difference, he claims that no violence has occurred if Christianity or other "value orientations" are left unrealized but only when "mental capacities," such as literacy, are deficiently actualized.

Galtung is making a major assumption here that needs to be examined. He seems to imply that literacy is essential for the good life but Christianity or any other value orientation is unessential precisely because there is a lack of consensus on these matters. But is it not the case that human beings often disagree about those things, such as religion, that are most important in life? Should one discount the importance of value orientations simply because they do not easily lend themselves to agreement or consensus? For if no violence is present when value orientations are left unrealized, then Galtung implicitly claims that one can achieve positive peace or the "good life" without actualizing any specific value orientation. In other words, he seems to suggest that positive peace or the good life need not include the implementation or actualization of some value orientation but, rather, only the actualization of mental capacities and bodily goods, such as literacy, food, clothing, and shelter. Is this plausible? Does it make sense to say that the good life can be achieved without some agreement about the underlying set of values that give life meaning and coherence? If everyone has food, clothing, and shelter and the ability to read, write, and think, but there is no agreement about what makes life worthwhile or meaningful, is this a condition of genuine peace or the fulfillment of the good life? It is these questions that draw a discussion of Galtung's notions of peace and violence into the wider political debate between liberalism and communitarianism.

The ongoing debate between liberals and communitarians focuses on the question of how best to organize society. There are, of course, important subtleties and nuances among different thinkers on each side of the debate, but here I will simply try to sketch out the basic contrast between the two views.

In general, liberals argue that the best way to organize society is to devise public procedures and state institutions that ensure freedom and fairness for all persons, and this goal is principally accomplished by bracketing out questions of the good life from the public domain. In other words, conceptions of the good life, such as the realm of religion, are confined to the private sphere. Public life is set up to allow each individual or group to pursue, within the limits of the law, its own conception of the good life. Liberalism, one might say, follows the adage "you do your thing and I will do mine." The goal of a liberal society is to maximize the opportunities of individuals and groups to pursue their own definitions of happiness. There are limits of course, namely, that one cannot harm or infringe on the neighbor's equal right to pursue his or her own view of the good life. The liberal state seeks to ensure that individuals have the opportunity to realize bodily goods (health and nutrition) and mental capacities (education and literacy). Value orientations, however, are a private matter and are left in the hands of individuals and private associations.

What is implicit in many if not all forms of liberalism is the assumption that conceptions of the good life are grounded merely in individual preferences. That is, they assume that one cannot rationally assess or judge one view of the good life to be superior to another and, therefore, the question of the good life must remain a matter of personal choice or preference. This assumption is illustrated by the liberal political theorist Bruce Ackerman when he says, "While everybody has an opinion about the good life, none can be known to be superior to any other. It follows that anyone who asserts that . . . his aims are intrinsically superior doesn't know what he's talking about."[8] What is clearly evident from Ackerman's remark is that conceptions of the good life are viewed merely as individual opinions or preferences, preferences that cannot be rationally or publicly evaluated. Hence, because it is assumed that views of the good life cannot be evaluated, liberals insist that the public domain must remain neutral toward them, if not totally independent from them. In sum, the ultimate aim or goal of society, according to political liberalism, is to provide the necessary goods and opportunities (nutrition, health care, education, etc.) that will enable individuals or groups to pursue their own differing conceptions of the good life.

Galtung's notion of structural violence exemplifies a liberal view of society. He accepts the liberal assumption that value orientations are nonrational preferences that are not, even in theory, susceptible to rational consensus. Thus, he excludes value orientations from his definitions and conceptions of peace and violence. Positive peace is achieved, he suggests, when we have ensured all individuals the opportunity to realize their potential in terms of bodily goods and mental capacities. The question of value orientations is left up to personal choice and preference.

In contrast to Galtung and liberalism, communitarians contend that the ultimate aim or goal of society is to foster genuine community through a shared understanding of the good life. Authentic human flourishing, they argue, requires a "thicker" set of commitments beyond the commitment simply to achieve bodily goods and mental capacities. The human individual cannot properly be understood, they contend, as an unfettered, autonomous agent who exists independently of all attachments and aims and who chooses his or her conception of the good life as a mere preference. As the communitarian philosopher Michael Sandel puts it,

We cannot regard ourselves as independent in this [liberal] way without great cost to those loyalties and convictions whose moral force consists partly in the fact that living by them is inseparable from understanding ourselves as the particular persons we are—as members of this family or community or nation or people, as bearers of this history, as sons and daughters of that revolution, as citizens of this republic. Allegiances such as these are more than values I happen to have or aims I "espouse at any given time". . . . To imagine a person incapable of constitutive attachments such as these is not to conceive an ideally free and rational agent, but to imagine a person wholly without character, without moral depth.[9]

Communitarians, such as Sandel, challenge the liberal notion that conceptions of the good life are merely matters of individual taste, preference, and opinion. Individuals cannot, they argue, simply choose a conception of the good life like a pair of shoes off the rack. On the contrary, it is our conception of the good life—our "constitutive attachments"—that defines our identity as individuals. It is our attachment to these constitutive convictions and our allegiance to particular communities, such as family, neighborhood, nation, or religion, that define who we are. In short, individuals exist in and are significantly constituted by their participation in community, and it is a shared value orientation among members of the community that is the basis of the good life (along with realization of bodily goods and mental capacities).

Adler's List of Necessary Goods for the Achievement of the Good Life

In order to clarify our understanding of these concepts and viewpoints more fully, let us look at a specific conception of the good life.[10] In his book *Reforming Education: The Opening of the American Mind*, the philosopher

Mortimer Adler attempts to elucidate what the American Declaration of Independence means when it states that all persons have a right to the "pursuit of happiness." Adler concludes that this means that each individual has "rights to the real goods that each of us needs in order to make good lives for ourselves."11 His reference to "real" goods denotes a distinction between those goods that are truly good for human beings and those merely perceived as such. Adler thinks human desires can be evaluated, which means that some are found to be authentically good while others are merely putatively good. Among those that are "real" or genuine goods, Adler identifies seven that he thinks every individual needs in order to make a happy or good life.

(1)   *the goods of the body*—such as physical health, bodily vigor, and the pleasures of sense.

(2)   *economic goods*—such as a decent supply of the means of subsistence, living and working conditions conducive to health, and opportunities for access to the pleasures of sense, the pleasures of play, and esthetic pleasures.

(3)   *political goods*—such as civil peace and political liberty, together with the protection of individual freedom by the prevention of violence, aggression, coercion, and intimidation.

(4)   *social goods*—such as equality of status and of treatment in all matters affecting the dignity of the human person.

(5)   *the goods of personal association*—such as family relationships, friendships, and loves.

(6)   *goods of the mind*—such intellectual virtues as knowledge, understanding, a modicum of wisdom, both practical and speculative, together with such goods of the mind's activity as the liberal arts—the skills of inquiry and of learning, the habits of critical judgment and creative production.

(7)   *goods of character*—such moral virtues as temperance, fortitude, and justice, all of which are firm habits of not yielding to wants that will get in the way of your acquiring the goods you need.[12]

Adler's conception of the good life, as evident from this list, involves a mixture of communitarian and liberal strands—a mixture, one might say, of Aristotle and Locke. With Aristotle and the communitarians, Adler contends that human desires and conceptions of the good life are not morally neutral or merely a matter of individual preference. On the contrary, desires and conceptions of the good life can be morally evaluated. For instance, Adler defines the "goods of character" as those habits or virtues that enable individuals to discern which wants or desires should be fulfilled (genuine goods) and those that should be resisted (putative goods). In relation to Galtung, this would mean that structural violence occurs only when authentic potentials are inhibited (those potentials necessary for the achievement of the good life) not merely when declared or putative potentials are inhibited. Hence, when Galtung defines violence as the "cause of the difference between the potential and the actual, between what could have been and what is," Adler would want to know what potential one has in mind—is it a potential that genuinely contributes to the good life, or is it one that only appears to be good or contribute to the good life? For example, in reference to social goods, structural violence genuinely occurs, Adler might say, when persons are treated without dignity, as less than human—as, for example, the Okies are in *The Grapes of Wrath*. In a society where some persons are systematically treated as second-class citizens, structural violence is present. However, if one of the Okies insisted that his or her potential to become rich failed to actualize, I think Adler would contend that this is not a case of structural violence. As long as that person was given an equal opportunity, treated with human dignity, and had a "decent supply of the means of subsistence," Adler would likely argue that this person's failed quest for riches does not constitute a case of structural violence. In short, not every potential realization carries equal moral weight or significance.

Alternatively, in company with Locke and the liberals, Adler defines the good life in individualistic terms. His list of seven items identifies those "real goods that each of us [as individuals] needs in order to make good lives for ourselves." Whereas his emphasis on "real" goods places Adler in company with Aristotle and the communitarians, his emphasis on the fulfillment of the individual places him in company with Locke and liberalism. Notice, for instance, that Adler does not include the goods of community in his list. Rather, he speaks only of the goods of personal association, such as family, friends, and loves. Moreover, his definitions of political and social goods focus on the protection of individual freedom and the status and dignity of the individual. This individualistic emphasis of "Lockean liberalism" is summed up well by Robert Bellah and his colleagues. "In our great desire to free the individual for happiness," Bellah says, "we Americans have tried to make a social world that would serve the self."[13] Adler's list is designed to "serve the self"—to guide the individual in his or her path to fulfillment. Unlike communitarians, Adler does not seem to locate and define the individual as a participant in a larger whole—in a community that provides constitutive meaning and loyalties for the life of the individual. Differently stated, Adler does not define the good life in terms of participating in a community that shares a common value orientation, a common view of the good life. Another way to approach this issue is to ask whether a group of individuals who possessed all seven goods on Adler's list would constitute a peaceful and harmonious community or would there still be sources of conflict and potential violence? Would they coexist in tension or in harmony?

AN ANALYSIS OF THREE FILMS

The Grapes of Wrath

The Grapes of Wrath powerfully portrays issues and conflicts of class, capitalism, and culture. Set during the depression and dust-bowl years of the 1930s, it is a story about an Oklahoma family that is forced off their farm and who then, in the face of hardship, journey to the "promised land" of California in search of peace, security, and a new home. However, after arriving in California, they find not the good life they anticipated but, rather, further forms of structural violence and new forms of class and cultural bigotry. In Galtung's terms, their actual realizations (and that of other Oklahoma migrants) are held below their potential realizations due to the various forms of structural violence they encounter both in Oklahoma and California. For instance, in the midst of drought and crop failure in Oklahoma, it is the "invisible powers," namely, the banks and corporations, that force them off the land—literally bulldozing their house—when they are unable to make their rent or mortgage payments. Their former farm is then merged into a large corporate farm, which has become economically advantageous due to advancing technology and equipment.

From the perspective of the family members, advance farm technology and corporate farming are direct threats to their way of life. Their conception of the good life is defined by a strong link between family and land, denoting, for them, a stable community. The good life, declares Tom, the son played by Henry Fonda, is when you "eat food you raise and live in the house you build." But the structural forces of a capitalistic economy bring this connection between family and land to an end. Consequently, in the face of homelessness and joblessness, they are drawn to California by leaflets that advertise good paying jobs for farm workers. Yet, when they arrive there, they find that the supply of workers greatly exceeds the demand for labor, thus, driving down wages to near or below poverty levels. Hence, once again, their capacity to realize the necessary bodily and mental components of a good life are restricted by systemic structures.

In terms of Adler's list, they are denied or have limited access to at least four of the seven necessary goods: (1) goods of the body—the grandmother's health quickly deteriorates during the arduous journey to California and she dies in the back of their rickety truck; (2) economic goods—the lack of decent wages leads the Oklahoma migrants to live in dirty and unsanitary camps; (3) political goods—the Oklahoma migrants have little or no political or economic power in California and, thus, they are at the mercy of the local police and hiring bosses. They are threatened and beaten by them at will; (4) social goods—their lack of social status and equal treatment are exemplified by the subhuman way that they are viewed by the people they meet in and on their way to California. In a vivid scene at a gas station along the road in Arizona, two cleanly attired gas station attendants look at the rickety truck and the dirty condition of the family and say, "those Okies aren't human." And once in California, they hear that we "don't want any more Okies here!" At one point, one of the migrants cries out, "our people are treated like pigs!"

In contrast to the portrayed inhumanity and structural violence of capitalism, Steinbeck offers an alternative vision of cooperative socialism. This socialistic vision of community is summed up by Tom when he states that "everyone has a piece of a big soul not a separate individual soul." The family eventually finds a trace of this vision of the good life in the form of a federally sponsored workers' camp. The camp, organized in a socialistic manner, is run by the workers themselves. It is sparkling clean, with showers and indoor plumbing, and generates a sense of self-respect and community among the workers and their families. This sense of community leads them to sponsor a square dance that is open to workers from all the surrounding areas and camps. In the face of this successful socialistic experiment, the local police and hiring bosses try to incite violence at the dance as a pretext for shutting down the camp. The workers catch wind of their plan and derail it by preventing the physical violence.

In sum, what are the underlying forms of violence in this film and what is its conception of peace? As suggested, the film illustrates various forms of structural violence and shows how structural violence often gives rise to physical violence. Its vision of peace is one of socialistic harmony where decent wages and decent housing are accompanied by a cooperative spirit among workers and families. In agreement with communitarians, the film seems to identify and locate individuals as participants in the larger whole of community. As Tom says, "everyone has a piece of a big soul not a separate individual soul." But with Galtung and liberal theorists, the emphasis seems to be on bodily goods and mental capacities more than on a common value orientation.[14]

Do the Right Thing

Spike Lee's *Do the Right Thing* portrays life in a New York neighborhood on a scorching hot summer day in the 1980s. The neighborhood is racially and ethnically mixed with the residents consisting mostly of blacks, some

Latinos, and one young white man from Boston. The businesses featured in the neighborhood are Sal's Italian pizzeria, a Korean grocery store, and a black radio station. Economic issues in the film are tied to racial issues. The customers are mostly black, but the proprietors are Italians and Koreans who live outside the neighborhood and, consequently, who channel their income and profits away from the neighborhood.

Once again, structural violence in this film eventually leads, in the climactic scene, to physical violence. The connection between structural and physical violence is reflected in the film's opening song, "Fight the Powers that Be," by the rap group Public Enemy.

In terms of Adler's list, the blacks in the neighborhood lack economic, political, and social goods. But the film also raises questions about the goods of character. For instance, three older black men, one of whom is apparently from the Caribbean, sit on the street corner across from the Korean grocer and debate why it is that Koreans find a way to save their money and buy businesses in a black neighborhood when blacks fail to do so. Is it due to some systemic injustice that prevents blacks from raising adequate capital, or is it due to a lack of industrious and virtuous character? Or both? The Caribbean American says, "[Either] Koreans are geniuses or your black asses are dumb." In another scene, Mookie, played by Spike Lee, argues with his sister about his attitude toward his delivery job at Sal's pizzeria and his responsibilities to his son, born to his Latino girlfriend, Tina. Mookie's sister tells him that he should not simply work to "get paid," but, rather, that he should take "care of [his] responsibilities."

The film powerfully portrays how conflicts in the business setting entail and are reflective of conflicts between racial and ethnic groups. For instance, in a pivotal scene that foreshadows the violence to come, a young black man walks into Sal's pizzeria and orders his usual slice of pizza. He complains about the price and the lack of cheese on the pizza. Then, after losing this debate with Sal, he sits down in a booth near some other black patrons. As he is about to take his first bite, he notices the photographs on the wall above the booth. All the pictures are of famous Italian Americans, such as Joe Dimaggio, Frank Sinatra, and Rocky Marciano. Above the pictures, Sal has titled the display the Italian-American "Hall of Fame." The young black man yells over to Sal, "how come there are no brothers on the wall?" Sal's tart response is: "you get your own pizzeria and you can put up whomever you want!" The black man retorts that Sal's customers are all black, not Italian Americans, and, therefore, that he should include some African Americans on the wall. Tensions rise as Sal defends his rights as a proprietor to celebrate and display his own ethnic and cultural identity while the young black man defends the rights of the African-American patrons to enjoy equal respect and dignity for their identity. Finally, as the tensions boil toward physical violence, the young black man is escorted out of the restaurant by a reluctant Mookie, who is trying to mediate between his boss and his friend. The young black man threatens to initiate a boycott of Sal's, which further increases Sal's anger. Outside, as Mookie tries to calm his friend, Mookie asks him not to jeopardize his job by starting a boycott. In response, his friend tells Mookie to "stay black."

This scene powerfully raises the contemporary question about the underlying source of human conflict and violence. Is the underlying source of conflict in this scene economic or cultural? How would Galtung, Adler, liberals, and communitarians respond to this scene? Is it wrong for Sal not to include non-Italians on his restaurant wall? Is the young black man right to demand "brothers on the wall" because African Americans are the ones who constitute Sal's business? Is the dispute about bodily goods, mental capacities, or value orientations? What would bring about peace in this situation? To empower blacks to own their own businesses so that they could have their own African-American "Hall of Fame?" To persuade Sal that he should either not celebrate his cultural identity or that he should do so only in the private confines of his home or neighborhood? Or should Sal be persuaded that he should celebrate the identities and cultures of his customers as much as his own? What is at stake is not simply the equality and dignity of individual persons, as suggested by Adler's category of social goods, but, rather, the identity and dignity of communities and their cultural values. Thus, the conflict, it seems, is more about value orientations than it is about bodily goods or mental capacities. If so, does this scene challenge Galtung's definition of positive peace, which tends to downplay the importance of value orientations?

Finally, in the film's climactic scene, the young black man returns to Sal's with another character, Radio Raheem, a young, strong, silent black man who carries around a large "boom box" blasting rap music at full volume. Sal has previously warned him to turn off the box before entering the restaurant. This time the simmering anger boils over; Sal smashes the box with a baseball bat and then a fight breaks out between Sal and Radio Raheem. As the fight moves out into the street, Radio Raheem has Sal on the ground in a choke hold. But then the police arrive—two white officers who are perhaps Italian Americans. They pull Radio Raheem off of Sal and then put Radio Raheem into a death-inducing choke hold. By this time, the neighborhood has gathered around and once they realize that Radio Raheem is dead, Mookie leads a revolt against Sal's restaurant and they smash and burn it down.

In this scene the police clearly used excessive force, which led to the unnecessary and unjust death of Radio Raheem. In Adler's terms, it reflected the African-American community's lack of political goods—its lack of protection from aggression and intimidation from the state and its authorities. In short, it reflected their lack of political equality and liberty. But prior to the police's arrival, what was the underlying source of conflict and violence between Sal and Radio Raheem? Was it an unfortunate ventilation of anger due to larger societal forces of racial and economic injustices? In other words, was it due to a lack of justice—due to a lack of adequate distribution of bodily goods and mental capacities? Or was it due to a conflict between different cultural values—due to different conceptions of what makes life good and/or civil? Is Radio Raheem's blasting box, at root, a form of protest against inequality and injustice or is it also reflective of some deeper cultural conception of the good life? Would Radio Raheem gladly give up his high-volume music if social conditions and opportunities for African Americans were significantly improved or is it more than a form of protest? Since liberalism seeks to maximize the freedom of all individuals to pursue their own conception of the good life, how would liberals respond to this situation? Would they tell Radio Raheem that he can only play his loud music in the confines of his own living space? How would communitarians respond? Would they say that Radio Raheem's music is meant to be communal and, thus, shared with others in the community? But what does one do when there are different communities (Italian Americans, African Americans, and Latinos) with their different conceptions of the good life in the same neighborhood?

A Raisin in the Sun

A Raisin in the Sun depicts a black family (the Youngers) on Chicago's Southside during the 1950s. The family consists of a mother (Mama), her daughter (Beneatha), her son (Walter), Walter's wife (Ruth), and their young son (Travis). The family lives in an overcrowded apartment with a bathroom down the hall, which is shared by other residents. Walter and Ruth work as domestic staff for a wealthy white family in the Chicago area. Mama has recently retired from domestic work because she is expecting the arrival of a large life insurance check, following the death of her husband. The anticipation of this check becomes the driving force of the film as the family members anxiously anticipate their coming "riches." It soon becomes clear that each family member has a different idea of how the money ought to be spent and these differences reflect their different conceptions of the good life.

Walter, for instance, wants to use the money to invest in a new liquor store with two other men. He seeks the responsibility and pride of ownership. He is tired of not being able to provide for his family as he thinks a man ought to do.

"Money is life!" exclaims Walter in a moment of frustration and anger. Ruth, on the other hand, wants a new house where they can all have adequate space to live and grow. Beneatha, in contrast, wants to use the money so that she can afford to go to medical school. She seeks to become a respected secular professional. She disparages the traditional Christianity of her mother and espouses a separatist African vision. In response, Mama insists that there will be "no disparaging of God" in her house. And contrary to Walter's wishes, Mama insists that no money will be spent on a liquor store.

Needless to say, tensions and conflicts between family members rise during this time of anticipation. How then does one reconcile the conflicts between them and their differing conceptions of happiness and the good life? If the money enables the family to actualize whichever potentials they choose (new business, medical school, or new home), how should they decide which potentials *ought* to be realized? Put simply, liberals think this question cannot be directly or rationally answered so they seek to mitigate conflict by insisting that all persons have an equal or fair opportunity to voice their views. Perhaps liberals would say that the money should be divided evenly among the family members so that they can each pursue, at least in part, their own differing views of the good life. This, they hope, would eliminate or diminish the potential for conflict and violence. Communitarians, in contrast, might suggest that the family (community) identify those fundamental values that orient their common life together and then proceed to make decisions based on those core values. In other words, they would suggest attempting to identify a common conception of the good life.

Finally, when the check arrives, Mama decides to put some of the money away for Beneatha's tuition and then, with the rest, to buy a new house for the entire family. But she decides to trust Walter by giving him the tuition money to take to the bank. He ends up investing and losing part of it in a liquor store deal that turns out to be a scam. With the remaining money, Mama buys a new house in a white suburb, as it offered the best and most affordable value. As the family is busy packing for the move, they are visited by a spokesman from the new neighborhood who, while espousing all the ideals of integration, offers to pay the family a large sum of money not to move into the neighborhood. The family seems to rally around one another in the face of this prejudice, and, defiantly, the film ends by showing them moving into the new house and neighborhood.

Common Theme

This theme of exclusion from community is found in all three films. In *The Grapes of Wrath*, most of the Californians want to keep the "Okies" out.

"We don't want anymore Okies here," they exclaim. In *Do the Right Thing*, a group of young blacks tell the young white man from Boston that he should go back to Boston. And in *A Raisin in the Sun*, the white homeowners seek to pay the black family to stay out of their neighborhood. In all three of these cases, it seems that residents of the neighborhood or area are trying to maintain the form of life and the identity of the community that existed prior to the new or recent arrivals. They want to maintain what they perceive as the status quo—the identity of the community and the substance of its values that existed before. Perhaps in all three of these cases, the residents are morally wrong for seeking to resist or discourage the new arrivals. Yet, the underlying question needs to be addressed, particularly in the context of the 1990s when international immigration and even interstate migration are central and divisive issues. Is it always morally wrong to want to maintain the status quo of a community and, thus, to discourage new arrivals? If so, what are the reasons or bases for this conclusion? Might one argue that human existence is, by nature, dynamic and evolving and, therefore, that one ought always to embrace change rather than resist it? That one has a moral obligation to seek maximal creativity and dynamism and, thus, to embrace change? But is change always creative rather than destructive? As a precautionary measure, can residents accept new arrivals but insist that they conform to the norms and values of the community? Or would this be wrong precisely because it embraces stasis rather than dynamism? In sum, is a pluralistic community morally or normatively better than a relatively homogeneous one? Are integrated communities normatively better than distinct ethnic neighborhoods?

The American cultural and intellectual historian Christopher Lasch argues in favor of distinct ethnic neighborhoods. Drawing on Josiah Royce's "philosophy of loyalty," Lasch argues that distinct communities with specific loyalties and identities are more likely to foster peace and tolerance than integrated communities that lack distinct identities and specific loyalties. People who are themselves loyal to a specific community, Lasch contends, are more likely to respect the loyalties of others than those who feel no loyalty to anything beyond themselves.[15] Hence, Lasch might argue that it was not altogether morally wrong for the Californians, the blacks, or the whites to resist the infusion and integration of outsiders.

In response to Lasch, one might argue that, in espousing the virtue of specific loyalties, Lasch does not pay sufficient attention to the adequacy of the objects of peoples' loyalties. Loyalty to race, ethnicity, class, gender, or even religion can easily become idolatrous and, thus, a demonic force in human society. As the American ethicist and theologian Reinhold Niebuhr says, "it is not possible to appreciate and preserve particularity and uniqueness whether individual or national, without either bringing it into relation with, and subordination to, an ultimate centre and source of meaning or allowing the particular and the unique value to become itself an imperialistic centre of ultimate meaning."[16]

Alternatively, if one concludes that it is sometimes permissible to resist the infusion of outsiders into a neighborhood, what are the bases for this judgment? Might one argue that it is always wrong to resist inclusion of people based on those aspects of their identity that they cannot change, such as race, gender, ethnicity, and perhaps socioeconomic standing and religion? Thus, the white homeowners in *A Raisin in the Sun* were morally wrong for seeking to keep out the black family simply because they are black. And likewise, the young blacks in *Do the Right Thing* were wrong to tell the young white man to go back to Boston. So, too, one could say that the Californians in *The Grapes of Wrath* were wrong to resist the Oklahoma migrants based on their socioeconomic status. But what if the young man from Boston was a member of the Ku Klux Klan? Would that be legitimate grounds for encouraging him to move back to Boston? Are there any legitimate grounds for discouraging the inclusion of outsiders into a community? Is there a moral distinction between the act of discouraging outsiders from coming in and the act of encouraging those who are already there to leave? In other words, is there a moral difference between tight immigration policies and "ethnic cleansing"? Is the relevant difference one of physical violence or are both cases equal forms of structural violence?

In one of the ironies of history, southern Californians today find themselves somewhat in the role of "Okies" as they make their exodus out of California into surrounding western states, such as Oregon, Washington, and Colorado. Residents of cities, such as Portland, Seattle, and Denver, are as reluctant to receive the migration of southern Californians as the Californians were to receive those migrating from Oklahoma sixty years ago. Residents of Portland, Seattle, and Denver want to maintain the quality of life that existed prior to the new influx. The influx of Californians has pushed up the price of homes to unaffordable levels, increased traffic and congestion in the cities, and introduced different sets of cultural values into the life of these communities. A student of mine from the Seattle area told me that there is a billboard along the interstate that encourages Californians, only half-kiddingly, to turn around and go home. Is it justified for residents of these cities to resist such an influx? If so, is their resistance different from the resistance the Californians showed to the Okies? Does it make a moral difference that the Okies were viewed as poor and inhuman whereas contemporary Californians are viewed as rich and, perhaps, culturally shallow?

How would communitarians respond to this set of questions? Would they concur with Lasch that distinct communities with specific loyalties are more likely to foster genuine tolerance and social harmony? In contrast, would liberals always argue in favor of the freedom and rights of individuals to move wherever they wanted? Would they always judge resistance to outsiders as a form of prejudice and intolerance? In the contemporary debates about welfare reform and interstate migration, these questions and issues are very much in play. For instance, the mayor of Madison, Wisconsin, a devoted political liberal, now questions the influx of Chicagoans coming to Wisconsin looking for better welfare benefits. As Dirk Johnson of the *New York Times* describes it:

Even [Madison] Mayor Paul Soglin, who earned his liberal stripes in the anti-establishment politics of the 1960's . . . now talks of "finite limits of resources" for the poor. He warns against "the duplication of old ghetto neighborhoods" with the same problems that families came to Madison to escape. "We're like a lifeboat that holds 12 people comfortably," Mr. Soglin said. "We've got about 16 in it now, and there's a dozen more waiting in the water. Since we're already in danger of going under, what can our community be expected to do?"[17]

As illustrated by this account, these are indeed complicated issues for liberals as well as communitarians. In this chapter, I have attempted to set forth, explain, and interpret some key concepts, such as structural violence, that can help us better understand the relationships among violence, peace, and the good life. I have also attempted to apply these interpretive "tools" to three American films as a way to illuminate some important issues and raise some thoughtful and provocative questions.

NOTES

1. Readers may choose to begin with the discussion and analysis of the films in part two and then refer back to the more theoretical discussion in part one as needed or desired. Though part two presupposes the detailed explanations and discussions of part one, it is sufficiently clear on its own terms to enable readers to begin there if they so desire.

2. Johan Galtung, "Violence, Peace, and Peace Research," in *Essays in Peace Research,* Vol. 1, *Peace: Research, Education, Action* (Copenhagen, Christian Ejlers, 1975), 110.

3. Ibid.

4. Ibid., 110–11.

5. Ibid., 111.

6. Ibid.

7. Ibid., 112.

8. Bruce A. Ackerman, *Social Justice in the Liberal State* (New Haven, CT: Yale University Press, 1980), 11.

9. Michael J. Sandel, *Liberalism and the Limits of Justice* (Cambridge: Cambridge University Press, 1982), 179.

10. At the beginning of one film workshop on the issue of structural violence and the good life, we gave students (both undergraduates and graduates) a brief survey asking them what goods they thought were necessary for the good life. We then used Adler's list as a means of focusing and furthering the discussion.

11. Mortimer J. Adler, *Reforming Education: The Opening of the American Mind* (New York: Collier Books, 1990), 85.

12. Ibid., 85–86.

13. Robert N. Bellah, et al., *The Good Society* (New York: Alfred A. Knopf, 1991), 85.

14. Or, alternatively, does the film suggest that the good life requires a shared value orientation, namely, one of humanistic socialism?

15. See Christopher Lasch, *The True and Only Heaven: Progress and its Critics* (New York: W.W. Norton & Co., 1991), 356f. for discussion of Royce and 496f. for a discussion of the Boston busing controversy of the 1970s as a particular historical example.

16. Reinhold Niebuhr, *The Nature and Destiny of Man,* Vol. 1, *Human Nature* (New York: Charles Scribner's Sons, 1941; reprint 1964), 88.

17. Dirk Johnson, "Larger Benefits and Safer Streets Attract Chicagoans to Wisconsin: Rethinking Welfare/Interstate Migration," *New York Times*, May 8, 1995, 1.

2

She Doth Protest Too Much, or Does She? An Essay on Gender, Violence, and Domination

Jean C. Robinson

In Israel, Women in Black gathered weekly on street corners in Tel Aviv and elsewhere to protest continuing state-sanctioned violence against Palestinians. In Argentina, Las Madres de los Desparecidos circled the plaza and sought investigations into the disappearance of thousands of young men and women during the reign of the Generals. In Nevada in the early 1960s and in Britain in the late 1970s, women organized massive sit-ins and demonstrations against nuclear proliferation. In South Africa, black women organized in the fight to overturn apartheid. And yet, women throughout the world are perceived as apolitical and uninvolved in social protest.

Closer to home, women have engaged in active resistance to violence, whether it be lynching, rape, or unjust wars. Within their homes, some women have sought to fight back against husbands who beat them and abused their children. And yet, women throughout the world are perceived as passive, politically apathetic, and inherently non-violent.

Popular culture would have us believe that all women are dominated, and that, thus subjected, no woman has agency. No woman can control her life or can act in her own defense. We think of women, as I will argue, as being in need of protection, which assumes, of course, that all women need protectors. The cultural stereotype of being female in the United States, which in our ethnocentrism we have expanded to women everywhere, is one of a weak, apolitical, nonresistant victim. Things just "happen" to women and to the people they love. Women do not fight, nor do they resist, nor do they seek to change their larger environment.

Think for a moment about how the media depicted Nicole Brown Simpson, the murdered estranged wife of O.J. Simpson. With no access to evidence from the murder or the marital relationship, from the beginning, Simpson was presented as young, beautiful, dependent, and weak. She ended up dead, so we are told, because she was a victim, unable to fight back, unable to escape—a violent marriage, a battered relationship, a love that destroyed her. We don't know, and probably will never know, in what ways Nicole Brown Simpson was strong, how she fought back, whether she resisted. But the way she was presented in the summer of 1994 fit with our expectations. It is almost as if we will not allow ourselves to see the ways in which women can protect themselves, the ways in which women can be proactive in stopping or preventing harm.

In film and television, most women are subject objects: they are objectified as bodies that produce children and satisfy men. They seldom have anything important to say, much less anything significant to do. The few times women are allowed to break out of this stereotype come when they are protecting their children (e.g. when maternal love forces the woman to strike back as in *Burning Bed)* or when they are venting their rage against former male lovers, as in *Fatal Attraction*, or at men in general, as in *Basic Instinct* or *Thelma and Louise.* Otherwise, if the mainstream popular media were to describe reality in full, we would have to believe that women accept abuse wherever they live, be it a Beverly Hills hotel penthouse (*Pretty Woman*) or a scrappy Mississippi town (*Mississippi Burning*). It is difficult to find women in film who resist domination, whose motivation to action comes from beyond intimate relationships, who see themselves as political agents. Indeed the most recent antifeminist popular take on women is that modern American feminism has told women they are passive victims, that feminism in its fulsome power in the 1970s and 1980s created a victimization of the female. The moral, we are told, is that women need to reject both this victim mentality[1] and the feminism that gave birth to it. In their place, women are to seek refuge in loving relationships, to accept protection from those (their husbands, their fathers, their police, their soldiers) whose appropriate role is to protect women, and to revel in their roles not as helpless victims but as well-adjusted females.

I want to claim here that the stereotype that seems to prevail in feature films and popular publishing denies the existence of strong women (and groups of women) who resist domination.[2] It ignores the active, sometimes (dare I write it) even violent political involvement of women. It maintains a myth that women only act as mothers. Finally, it blames feminism for a perceptual condition that precedes feminism in all its varieties: this condition is the bedrock upon which the hegemony of an ideology of male power is maintained.

We do our students a disservice if we fail to confront them with the stereotypic ways in which genders are presented in the popular media. Certainly we all know women who are strong, women who have been politically active, women who are willing to fight. And lest we forget, we also know men who lack courage, men who are politically apathetic, men who are victims! But how to overcome the images in film, and indeed the unconsciously presented "fact" in our texts, that masculine gender is highly associated with political activity, violence, and commitment beyond ourselves and those we love? How can we change a discourse that starts with certain assumptions about what women are and what men are? Part of the project here is to acknowledge that our discussions about violence, about peace, and about fulfilling dreams will be more grounded if we can move away from gendered assumptions about violence. This is a large task, and in this short chapter, my intention is to suggest approaches that may be useful in shaking up our ideas about both gender and violence.

There is a second strand weaving through the text: that is the role of feminisms as agents of mobilization and social change and the responsibility of feminisms as critical social stands from which to interrogate the discourses of victim, agency, and resistance. This is not to claim that all acts of resistance by women are feminist, nor that only women can engage in feminist practice. Rather I propose that feminist standpoints provide opportunities to examine political action, resistance, and violence through lenses that foreground much that has been out of focus.

My standpoint here is as a feminist trained in political science. I have taught women's studies for two decades; I also teach about revolutions. I have a respect for the need for active opposition to domination. I do not believe that all violence is "bad"; some violence I would argue is necessary and justified. I do not believe that one "sex" is better than the other, nor more peaceful than the other, nor "naturally" more ethical or moral than the other.[3] (Nor am I willing to subscribe to the idea that there are only two sexes; but for convenience, we'll keep it to the two commonly accepted forms for this paper.) I do not believe that all women are victims.

I do, however, believe that political and social systems around the globe are structured in ways that advantage certain characteristics and that being female is not generally a characteristic that is advantaged. Indeed, in many social systems, the economic patterns and the political arrangements seem specifically designed to ensure that most women are subordinate to most men. To write this seems to be a mild position to take on the issue: to say that women are not generally advantaged veils what that means in the lives of women and men. Women receive less food, less health care, less education, less money, less political voice, less access to weapons, less security than men. In poverty, men suffer and women suffer, but usually women suffer more. My feminism is a recognition of this suffering and a claim that we have a responsibility to dismantle systems that are founded on such domination and suffering.

GENDER MYTHS: WOMEN'S MORAL QUALITIES AND APOLITICAL BEHAVIOR

In this brief chapter, I want to address the ways in which we can begin to explode that pervasive theme of woman as apolitical victim. Let me posit three broad stereotypes about women's moral qualities and political behavior. I will address each of these in terms of how gender is implicated in discussions of war and peace, violence, and domination. I will suggest films that work to sustain those stereotypes as well as films that may begin to break down such codes. This can then serve as a guide for developing ways to confront the rigidity of gender in issues touching on violence.

Myth 1: Women Are Inherently Nonviolent

Virginia Woolf in *Three Guineas* (1938) said that to "fight has always been the man's habit, not the woman's. Law and practice have developed that difference, whether innate or accidental." Modern sociologists argue that we teach males that to be a man is to practice violence, at least a certain kind of violence, in certain kinds of places, against certain kinds of people. It may be important that boys are showered with toys that elicit violent behavior and are entertained by games that require teamwork as well as a "we vs. them" mentality.[4] But it is not only the toys and games that we give boys. After all, girls are not just *not boys*. Rather, we encourage certain kinds of behaviors in girls as well. We reward them for acting feminine and for avoiding (or at least disengaging) from competition and violence. Study after study suggests that girls are encouraged to work out their differences in play by compromise and that when anger or violence seems imminent, girls step away from the activity. Boys on the other hand are encouraged to play to win, to fight out differences, to stick up for their principles, and to see the conflicts through to the end.[5]

Our society and most other western societies assume that females have a natural role as mothers and that there is something intrinsically peaceful about maternity. Certainly strands of feminist thought as well as popular assumptions of women's attitudes toward violence, war, and peace are founded on sex-based stereotypes. They accept the idea that women are supposed to be weak and dependent in order to be feminine. The logical consequence of this is that women must then rely on some gendered being other than other females in order to secure their existence: men must be constructed as their protectors and providers; otherwise females cannot grow up to be the feminine women we want them to be. The further corollary of this gender role construction of femininity reinforces heterosexuality for women (because women need men to do their fighting for them and to protect them from others) and insists that any violent activity of women can only be an outcome either of the attempt to preserve peace and protect children or of femininity run amok. In popular feature films, such as *Fatal Attraction*, the violence perpetrated by Glenn Close on Michael Douglas and his family only makes sense as competition between women over a man, as finally the only option for a woman desperately and destructively in love. Close's possessiveness actually reaffirms her femininity as outwardly her violence seems to work against it. Here is femininity understandable, albeit out of control. In other films in which female characters are allowed to lash out, their actions are justified not so much by the continuing violence done to them, but by threats of violence to their children. Thus, Farah Fawcett in *Burning Bed* (based on a true story) eventually kills her abusive husband in an effort to protect her family and children. In neither of these films are the female characters portrayed as resisting or trying to remodel sexual relations or the family. Rather the women's engagement with violence is an exception: brought on by provocation, it is neither "natural" nor does it arise out of other than domestic, intimate relationships. Underpinning these characterizations is a bedrock belief in the natural peacefulness of the female we have gendered as women.

Myth 2: Men Are the Protectors, Women Are the Protected

Our modern culture confronts us with a fundamental dichotomy: women are presumed to be peaceful, but they live in a violent world. Thus, women (and those they are responsible for, i.e., children) require protection. It is to men that women are to turn for protection, although apparently it is also men who create the need for protection. The culture of femininity projects an image of women who only resort to violence in extraordinary situations; the culture of masculinity is framed by a discourse that links it simultaneously with protection and violence. Popular culture and filmic images are pervaded by these two contrasting and symbiotic claims. I am not suggesting here that men, in real life, are the only and primary perpetrators of aggressive violence. Rather, I am suggesting that one of the lessons in learning what it means to be men and women is a lesson about aggression, protections, and protectors.

David Morgan, a British sociologist, argues that masculinities are socially constructed sets of distinctions that are strongly connected to the practice of legitimate violence.[6] Legitimate violence includes things such as soldiering, warfare, and police work, which boys early on learn are the roles they will assume in adulthood. Thus, even though western societies frequently voice concern about boys playing with guns and learning to be violent from video games, we also expect them to accept their aggressive role as adults. Morgan suggests that the legitimation of violence is part of the sexual division of labor: just as girls learn that they are supposed to be generous, warm, nonviolent, and caring, boys learn that they are to protect women and children, and that this requires violence (sometimes). After all, if there were no need for protecting women and children, there would be no rationale for men's continuing resort to legitimate violence. (In a modern civilized society, conflicts over property can be solved through negotiations and law.) Thus, both males and females learn their parts in the sexual division of social labor. These roles consequently reproduce the cultural constructions of masculinity and femininity that underlie the way violence and aggression are supposed to be organized.

The irony here is that civilized society has created a situation in which people need to be protected from the protectors. One of the common themes in Grade B movies is the lack of control of men with guns, whether they are in the "Wild West" or on the battlefield. Rape in war, rape out of war, men going berserk after war—all of these, from John Wayne flicks to the more recent *Heaven and Earth*, Oliver Stone's paean to war brides of Vietnam and posttraumatic stress disorder, affirm the irony. Judith Hicks Stiehm, a political scientist, argues that the sexual politics of militarization makes people into the protected or the protector.[7] The protected may be quite safe from attack: in films and real life, protectors can effectively threaten or use force on her behalf. But the flip side of this is that the protected are subject to attack from their protector. A woman typically does not use force; she is dependent on her protector, who not only provides for her, but may also beat her and abandon her. This story is told and retold in narratives of domestic violence whether they be in film or police blotters. It is not only soldiers who are to protect women; men in general are expected, perhaps trained, to be women's protectors. The role of the protected (always women and the young) signifies dependence, femininity, certainly less control, less power, and less privilege. And yet the protected retain some power: fundamentally, they are essential to the protector. They provide endorsement and justification for violence. And it is in the failure of the protector to protect them that women (and children) are given the right to exercise violence. Fawcett in *Burning Bed* can strike back at her husband; Susan Sarandon and Geena Davis in *Thelma and Louise* can attack men and defy the legal order because of men's failure to care for and protect them.

Here, of course, we come full circle back to the idea that women are not violent. If women have protectors who do their assigned job correctly, then it can easily appear that women are not violent. Men will be expected to fight wars in their name; men will be expected to stave off intruders and protect their women and children from violence. Indeed, think back to Michael Douglas in *Fatal Attraction*: part of his failure was his inability to protect his wife and children from this crazy woman. It is thus not only that women are the protected and nonviolent; it is also that men are the protectors and are supposed to be violent. Men, as the protectors, are responsible for themselves, for their dependents, for their nation. In that capacity, they are expected to be violent, if necessary, and thus to demonstrate their masculinity. The role of men in defending and protecting obliterates the responsibilities women have for violence as well. Indeed it is quite easy for women to appear less violent, but maybe it is just that their hands look clean because the killing is done for them, in their name!

Myth 3: Women Do Not Resist

Both the myth of women's nonviolence and the myth of men as protectors have a further logical consequence. That is, only men can engage in acts of resistance, whether on the personal or political level. If women are reified as victims, as those without access to power, or willingness to act violently except in extreme cases, then one can find no rationale for women acting consciously and thoughtfully as resisters. One would have to accept the proposition that women cannot act outside themselves, they cannot think themselves through to violent acts (even if necessary), that a woman cannot engage in what Simone de Beauvoir in her early feminist writing called transcendence: to engage in actions outside of herself and her body.[8]

The myth of women's lack of resistance stems from a number of misperceptions. One has to do with the way male and female activity and behavior are understood: if the majority of women's lives is spent in private domesticated spaces, and if that arena is defined as marginal to the public, politically significant arenas, then any actions women take to reshape private life will not be seen as resistance. Simultaneously, as Kate Soper relates, when masculine culture is defined as "the realm in which all non-conformity, rebellion and dissent from an established order of meanings and values has always and must necessarily find expression,"[9] then it is easy to focus only on men's doing in that cultural milieu. In fact, until very recently, it has been quite easy to assume that culture includes only male activity. Women are disenfranchised as it were. Here gender roles are confused with the real behavior of men and women as they live their lives. There is a failure to recognize all the ways in which women help to make history, in which women's resistance has brought about cultural change. As Soper continues, "We live in a world in which there are too many female breadwinners, male nurturers, feminist housewives and mothers, white middle class males teaching black feminist literature, in short, too many transgressions or confusions of gender in our everyday engagements for us not to feel that much of the former gender narrative is perversely and even cruelly anachronistic."[10]

The exception to the myth of women's lack of resistance has always been the archetype female who transforms herself into a male to engage in cultural activity and societal change. From Joan of Arc to George Sands, from women dressing up as young boys to fight in wars, to women revolutionaries who were accused of losing their femininity, these exceptions stand in tribute to the difficulty in getting society to accept women as active participants in moving and shaking their worlds. Women who do resist continue to be portrayed in literature and popular culture as odd exceptions, precisely those women who do not fit the normal expectations of womanhood.

VIOLENCE AND GENDER

The reality of women's lives around the globe does not fit the image of protected, unresistant subjects. Katie Roiphe and Camille Paglia to the contrary, many women are dominated; many women are subjects; many women are victims. They were not made so by feminism. No question about that. The most recent data published by the United Nations demonstrates the extent to which women across continents do not have control over their bodies, their choices, their lives. For instance, on the basis of data from 1990, "three quarters of women aged 25 and over in much of Africa and Asia are still illiterate";[11] girls have higher mortality rates than boys in a large number of countries and are more likely to be deprived of protein-rich foods than boys. As a result, a majority of women in developing countries are malnourished because women require three times as much iron a day as adult males, but they do not have access to the foods that would prevent anemia. "In many countries, it is still the custom for adult women and young children to eat after the men have had their fill, leaving them with less of the more nutritious foods. This tendency for girls and women to eat less food (or food with less nutritional value) is part of what diminishes the usually longer life expectancy of infant girls at birth compared with boys."[12]

The women who do survive into adulthood are likely to have to confront violence in their everyday lives as well. Although the UN notes that domestic violence, for example, is a worldwide phenomena, there is little statistical evidence that accurately reports on the amount of domestic violence to which women are subjected. The UN has reported that "violence in the home is common and that women are most frequently its victims."[13] And of course, then there is the violence that women and men, boys and girls are subjected to outside their homes. We often forget that although wars are supposed to be fought on battlefields, where men are to fulfill their roles as protectors, war often and usually spills over into homes and villages. Women and children are raped, their homes and fields are pillaged, and they, too, are subject to death by bullet, tank, and bomb. Eighty percent of all war refugees are women and children. Most women's experience of war, as for most children and the elderly, is not as combatants or activists, but as civilians caught in the crossfire. No firm statistics on this are available either, but the UN provides evidence that the number of civilians killed or disabled in war is climbing sharply. During the Second World War, about 50 percent of all casualties were civilians. The estimated ratio for civilian casualties in recent and ongoing wars now exceeds 80 percent; in individual cases, the rate is higher. In Lebanon, for instance, it is over 90 percent; in Bosnia, similar figures are probably accurate.[14]

War does yet more damage as well. In societies where women's status and welfare depend upon their relationship to men, war widows are often left without means to provide for themselves or their children. This also affects those who are effectively "widowed" when their husbands disappear: lost in action, missing, prisoners of war, and so on. Because women lose the support of their husbands and sons, they are no longer among the "protected," although in most societies they would be considered the "deserving" poor and therefore as qualified for assistance.

To deny that women are sometimes victims, often passive in the face of violence, and frequently apolitical would be to repudiate all of this evidence. We know though, from our own personal experiences, from the glimpses we learn through television of people like Chai Ling, (China) and Aung San Suu Kyi (Burma). Even from the simple confrontations between women and American corporations in the fight to protect neighborhoods, communities, and the earth that the common assumptions that women don't resist, that women aren't political, that women are always victims are falsehoods.

Knowing these truths from our own experiences and observations, we still maintain a public silence about the myriad ways in which women, like men, engage in political struggle. We are silent about women's resistance. The way we teach about politics and violence—in political science courses, in history courses, even in women's studies courses—is often to ignore women's roles, except as mothers unwilling to see their sons go to war, or as wives vainly trying to protect their families from sporadic and episodic violence from within and without. The cultural construction of gender with which we have become comfortable reifies women as mothers, passive in their resistance, concerned for their individual children. We maintain this set of myths by declining to interrogate its pervasiveness, by failing to offer alternative representations of women.

ALTERNATIVE REPRESENTATIONS OF WOMEN: RESISTANCE AND FILM

In this last section I want to suggest some films that can be useful in helping students to rethink gender, violence, and resistance. One of the primary aims here is to encourage a recognition of the realities of men's and women's lives, so that neither we as teachers nor our students presume that all men or all women can be expected to act in certain ways. The other primary aim is to facilitate a rethinking of what it means to resist. Let us broaden the idea of resistance so that it can include domestic resistance, nonviolent resistance, indeed all organized activities and personal actions that are aimed at trying to reclaim autonomy and control away from dominant powers.

Social scientists have long been concerned with the issue of public spaces: who has a place within them, what they are to encompass, who has control over its territory, borders, and norms, what is legitimate behavior within the public? The idea of the private, of what we have come to understand as the parameters of family life, is dependent on the breadth of the public. Roger Chartier, in his history of private life notes that "it is generally agreed that the limits of the private sphere depend primarily on the way public authority is constituted both in doctrine and in fact . . . on the authority claimed by the state."[15] This conceptualization of private life suggests that it is only understandable as a counterpart to the public sphere.[16] And though private life has a separate, often autonomous stance, it is not immune to institutional public control. Historically, and paradoxically, "private space only achieved autonomy when it had thoroughly internalized moral and social codes that had once been enforced by public authorities," and hence such autonomy was blighted.[17]

In a landscape where, as it is claimed, the public seems to dominate every aspect of society, how can women and men assert their autonomy? The most recent work of James C. Scott provides clues to the ways in which individuals and groups express resistance even in a totally dominated system. In his study *Domination and the Arts of Resistance: Hidden Transcripts*, Scott argues that the collective experience of groups with shared subjugation is that they develop "hidden transcripts." For Scott, these transcripts represent acts of resistance to domination; they are composed of speech, actions, and all other kinds of activities that are both outside the public transcript (what is publicly legitimate to do and say) and unacceptable to it (what is unacceptable to the hegemonic forces that control the public transcript and public domination). Scott looks at a variety of phenomena—terms of address, jokes, crowds, poaching, myths, fantasy, and so on. He is primarily interested in uncovering the counterhegemonic discourse of the dominated and, particularly, the "everyday forms of resistance" and the ways in which this daily resistance is sometimes transformed into open public opposition to domination.[18]

Scott's thesis leads the way to postulating that not only are there hidden transcripts that the subjugated use to express their opposition to state domination, but that there are particular "sites of resistance" as well. These sites, both physical and metaphysical, are places where subordinates are freer to express and share their resistance. In other words, there are places where people can speak their minds, places where people act out what they want, where they may at times even do what they want, despite or even because of the opposition to the state.

It seems to me that these sites of resistance must exist in different types of landscapes, in different places, depending on the structure of society and the penetrative ability of the state. But it would make sense to assume that those places that people consider most intimate, and thus closed off from the public world, are a good place to begin to look for these hidden sites of resistance. In other words, it is in private lives that we may find a new kind of resistance. One of the things we can do as teachers is to refocus students' attentions on the ways resistance is played out in domestic lives. Films are a wonderful way to get to that.

What kinds of film can we use to explore the ways in which women, in particular, and people in general, act in everyday ways, or extraordinary ways, to resist violence and oppression? Unfortunately looking to Hollywood doesn't give us much in the way of offering. But films such as *The Accused* (produced in 1988 and directed by Jonathan Kaplan), in which Jodie Foster portrays a woman gang-raped in a bar while the onlookers cheered (based on the real events in New Hampshire in the 1980s), reveal the multitude of ways in which rape affects the lives of women and men. *The Accused* explores the legal system and the peculiar notions of guilt and innocence attached to sexuality and sexual violence, the ways in which promiscuity and prior sexual histories can influence resistance and social understandings of rape, and the impact of specific male cultures that promote and encourage complicity among men.

Thelma and Louise (produced in 1991 and directed by Ridley Scott) earned a number of film awards. Hailed as the first "feminist-buddy" film, *Thelma and Louise* is a story about two working-class women who take to the open road when Thelma, played by Geena Davis, rebels against her abusive, domineering husband and follows Louise (played by Susan Sarandon), who suggests a respite from their male-dominated abusive lives. Of course, they find yet more male violence and abuse on the road and finally can only find release by total escape. Although in this popular film the women apply stereotypical male methods to the violence they encounter (guns aimed at groins and flames billowing out of trucks are their answer to violence) the film nevertheless provides an excellent opportunity to provoke discussion about male and female violence and about effective and ineffective methods of resistance.

There are, of course, less self-centered ways of resisting, such as is demonstrated in *The Official Story*, a 1985 film about the efforts of mothers and grandmothers in Argentina to discover what happened to their missing children. This is a political drama that focuses on the efforts of Les Madres de los Desaparecidos (the mothers of the "disappeared") who regularly marched in the main plazas of Buenos Aires to demand that the military government account for the torture and disappearance of their sons and daughters and to explain the subsequent adoption of their grandchildren by those who were friends of the regime (rather than by relatives). The film demonstrates the capacity of women to organize and resist in public arenas on the basis of personal and intimate relationships. It demonstrates the ways in which being a mother can motivate political action, as well as the various ways in which political systems can act as oppressive forces in the lives of families. Finally, it suggests quite powerfully that violence does not always beget violence: in this instance, on film and in the streets, women have shown that violence can be answered quite convincingly with peaceful resistance. In so doing, these women create new meaning for the idea of maternal politics.

Resistance, as Scott has shown on the basis of his observations in Southeast Asia, need not always be violent or aggressive. Indeed, just as telling jokes can serve as media for reproducing resistance, so, too, do family narratives and contemporary recastings of the past serve to reinvigorate resistance to the domination of mainstream cultures. In this way, subordinate or marginal cultures can be strengthened and recreated. Thus *Daughters of the Dust*, the 1992 directorial debut of Julie Dash, tells the story of the Gullah people, descendants of West African slaves, living on the Sea Islands off the coast of Georgia. Set in 1902, the family narratives, as told by five women of the Peazant family, endeavor to uncover the ways in which the family tradition and strength developed and survive in a world rapidly changing. Moving back and forth between tales of prostitution, rape, family unity, and women's central roles in maintaining and reproducing culture and religious beliefs, *Daughters of the Dust* is a moving and beautiful chronicle of the ways in which women as mothers, daughters, and workers sustain families and cultures in the face of barbarity and domination.

Resistance to violence takes a multitude of forms: telling stories to children, publicly demonstrating defiance, taking up arms if necessary. Just as remarkable and enduring are those efforts to uncover truths, to discover hidden histories of violence and oppression. The act of rediscovering history is part of family narratives, but it is also part of the public record. *The Nasty Girl*, a 1990 German film directed by Michael Verhoeven, shows the courage required of those who seek to continue resisting violence. Based on a true story, *The Nasty Girl* tells of the harassment and brutalization of a young girl who plans to write an essay on her hometown's history during the Third Reich for a national contest. Having discovered that the town leaders conspired to cover up atrocities against Jews during the war, the girl refuses to give up her research or to cover up the truth she exposes. Here we have a story of innocence meeting a conspiracy of violence: the response is an adamant plea for honesty and responsibility.

All of these films provide a new way of thinking about women, violence, and resistance. In some measure, these films demonstrate that women can act politically; that resistance can be domestic as well as public; and that women are not, and need not be, victims. A wealth of documentary films attest first to the ways in which women have been subjects of a gendered domination and then demonstrate the wealth of routes women have taken to redress those situations. A variety of films illustrate these points, including *Maids and Madams*, a 1986 documentary about the perverse relations between black and white women under apartheid in South Africa; *The Greenham Challenge*, a 1987 vivid retelling of the antinuclear movement led by women in Great Britain; *Women in War: Voices from the Front Lines*, a 1991 two-part award-winning film, which focuses on women living in war zones in Northern Ireland, Israel, El Salvador, and urban North America; and *Faith Even to the Fire: Nuns for Social Justice*, a 1991 documentary depicting U.S. nuns acting on the basis of the cry for justice rather than the commands of the

Church. Let it be clear that in these documentaries, as well as in the feature films, not only are women portrayed as agents rather than victims, they are also given a counterintuitive role as protectors, and they do resist.

These films enable our students to hear new voices and see new acts. In thus portraying women and men in alternative lights, they provide an opportunity to imagine gender in a less constricting way, to create new forms of resistance to violence, and to give value to the variety of ways in which women around the globe have transcended the narrow myths and archetypes that have long imprisoned them.

NOTES

1. Kate Roiphe, *The Morning After: Sex, Fear and Feminism on Campus* (Boston: Little, Brown and Company, 1993). Roiphe is incorrect both about the prevalence of rape and about the feminist movement's responsibility for sustaining the victim mentality. Rape happens regularly; not all women are victims nor see themselves that way. The victim mentality has not been emphasized by feminists. Actually, the opposite is true.

2. This stereotype exists in academic work as well. Our understanding of women in political science, until recently, was that they did not engage in violent political struggle; that they are not forceful agents resisting domination; and that the primary motivation for female political participation derives from their family life. See Murray Goot and Elizabeth Reid, *Women and Voting Studies: Mindless Matrons Or Sexless Scientism* (Beverly Hills: Sage Publications, 1975). Also see Rita Mae Kelly and Kimberly Fisher, "An Assessment of Articles about Women in the Top 15 Political Science Journals," *PS* 24, no. 3 (Sept 1993), 544–57.

3. See Carol Gilligan, *In a Different Voice.* (Cambridge: Harvard University Press, 1992). The popular interpretation of Gilligan in particular has been that she ascribes to women a "better" moral ethics. Rather, she argues that among the group of women she looked at, there may be a different set of priorities that help determine action than among men.

4. See, for instance, Lenore Weitzman's early study on *Sex Role Socialization* (Palo Alto, CA: Mayfield Publishing Company, 1979) as well as Carol Gilligan, Nora Lyons, and Trudy Hanmer, *Making Connections* (Troy, NY: Emma Willard School, 1989).

5. See M. F. Belenky, B. M. Clinchy, N. R. Goldberger, and J. M. Tarule, *Women's Ways of Knowing* (New York: Basic Books, 1986) and Sara Ruddick, *Maternal Thinking* (Boston: Beacon Press, 1989).

6. David Morgan, "Masculinity and Violence," in Jalna Hanmer and Mary Maynard, eds., *Women, Violence, and Social Control* (Atlantic Highlands, NJ: Humanities Press, International, 1987), 180–92, esp. 182–83.

7. Judith Hicks Stiehm, ed., *Women and Men's Wars*, special edition of *Women's Studies International Forum* (Oxford: Pergamon Press, 1982).

8. Simone de Beauvoir, *The Second Sex* (New York: Vintage, 1952).

9. Kate Soper, "Postmodernism and Its Discontents," *Feminist Review* (1991), 39, 105.

10. Ibid., 106.

11. *The World's Women: Trends and Statistics 1970–1990* (New York: United Nations Publications, 1991), 46.

12. Ibid., 58.

13. Ibid., 19–20.

14. Jeanne Vickers, *Women and War* (London: Zed Books, 1993).

15. Roger Chartier, *A History of Private Life,* Vol. 3, *Passions of the Renaissance* (Cambridge, MA: Harvard Belknap Press, 1989).

16. Elizabeth Goldsmith, "The Invention of Privacy," *The Women's Review of Books* 7 (9, June 1990), 24.

17. Ibid.

18. James C. Scott, *Domination and the Arts of Resistance* (New Haven, CT: Yale University Press, 1990), especially the discussion and table on the disguised, hidden forms of everyday resistance to state domination, 187–201.

_____ 3 _____

Exploring Sexual and Political Domination through Film

Barbara Allen

"All is fair in love and war" invites us to identify political violence with sexual violence, and our acceptance of this cliché is born out in reality daily. Viewers witnessed the fusion of sexual and political violence through metaphor during the 1992 television spectacle known as the Gulf War. Held captive, television audiences watched military personnel standing proudly beside phallic-shaped bombs painted with the message "Bend over, Saddam." While Air Force pilots spoke of their planes as their lovers, commentators were outraged about the "rape" of Kuwait. Listeners heard military engagements described in ways that emasculated the enemy, signaling their literal and figurative defeat as a victory for real men. The conjunction of sexual domination and warfare is more than metaphor, as references to actual campaigns of rape and pillage show. When Bosnian soldiers compel women to perform in brothels and Hindu and Muslim men in Bombay trade insults via the bludgeoning of the "enemy's women" for video cameras, sexual terror is integral to prosecuting the war.[1]

Framing the war message through these literal and figurative depictions of sexuality, media portrayals influence our understanding of combat and warrior. Fusing sex and violence in depictions of valiant and vanquished, this war narrative portrays two dimensions of sexuality: sexual potency and sexual terrorism. In this dichotomous depiction, winners are righteous, potent, and good, and losers are rapists, powerless, and evil. Because of this confusion, depictions of sexual domination make such displays of power appear inevitable, if not justifiable.

We address such "private" violence with public silence, leading to two results: (1) we apply the continuum of legitimate and illegitimate force, useful in discussions of political violence, inappropriately to our views of sexual violence; (2) we accept domination in private relationships as inevitable, creating a foundation for political relationships that is incongruous with the basic assumptions of self-government.

In nations that predicate political authority on strategies of dominance, obedience, control, and submission, authority exerted in the private sphere through gender dominance may accord with justifications for the state's dominance in the public sphere. In contrast, we imagine authority designed to prompt responses of self-organization and self-government ought to sever the link between sexual violence and political domination, viewing both as illegitimate uses of power. In democratic theory, we painstakingly distinguish between justified force—legitimate police powers and the just war—and illegitimate force, such as vigilantism or terrorism. Yet, even making such distinctions, the foundational culture of sexual terror pervades self-governing as well as authoritarian political cultures.

Sexual violence is experienced directly by some, but all of us experience the culture of sexual terror when we internalize the constant narrative of sexual predation. Popular visual media, from film to television news, frame public narratives in terms of our private movies of sexual violence, contributing to our internalization of a culture of sexual terror. Often popular media create this narration as a nexus of sexual violence and actual political violence. By recapitulating our personal wars as the public war story, we make sense of the traumatic events of political violence.

War requires deadly force, but killing in usual circumstances of civil society is taboo and traumatic. The logic that justifies the use of lethal force to maintain civil order cannot neutralize the effect of taking a human life in any simple way. The war story reconstructs acts of violence, achieving public sanction, relieving private censure. Iconographic storytelling, and the personal narrative of war made public, constructs the warrior, the war story, and the story of legitimate uses of deadly force.

The female gender construction functions in four ways in this reconstruction that legitimizes political violence. First, by acting as society's conscience, those in the female gender role are the "ears" that receive the war story. As the designated listeners, they not only must identify with the warrior, but also forgive his violence, and perhaps even deify him as hero.

The female gender role secondly functions in war as part of the required hierarchy of domination through force. In Surat and Bombay, India, the rape of women has become part of warfare as religious groups defile the enemy's "property," their women. Sexual terror in such cases becomes a weapon in war. Using sex and sexual violence as a key weapon of warfare establishes and maintains political power, equating sexual prowess, literally and figuratively with political power.

"Woman" as a gendered social construction also legitimizes political violence in a third way, by serving as sex object, in service to servicemen. Some analysts suggest that this function of women was supplanted by the sexualized technology and the thrill of high tech that we witnessed in Vietnam and Operation Desert Storm.[2] Unfortunately, the domination of the enemy through his women has not been replaced by technology; nor has the rhetoric that ties sexual dominance to political power been supplanted.

Finally, "woman" operates symbolically in the political violence of war. The strength (sexual potency) of the victor (or at least the self-described winner) becomes metaphoric and sexualized, resulting in the masculinization of war. Loss, the other side of this equation, feminizes the "loser" and valorizes the victor as "super male." This "Feminization of Loss," as Susan Jeffords calls it, is necessary for maintaining a core rule of patriarchy: men win, and only women lose.[3] The victors feminize the enemy, the losers; and the victor's inherent right to dominate the losers (described now as women) is exhibited in another form of violence, rape. Klaus Theweleit argues that this rule of patriarchy is so basic to governance, that with a lost war, "you will have no resurrection, re-erection, re-election. You will not be a man again, you will not be in control of all the things that have to be in control to make you feel like a natural winner, unless you've got a replay on the war machine; a replay you win."[4]

The backlash against women and peace activists during the Vietnam era was understood by Jeffords and Theweleit as America's method of re-winning the Vietnam War. They postulate that this replay eventually led to Operation Desert Storm and its particular construction of maleness. This construction of a gendered reality explains the necessity to sexualize war in order to maintain political and patriarchal authority, suggesting sexual domination is integral to political authority. Public and private war movies bear testimony to this tale.

The unintended fusion of political and sexual violence can be seen as a pervasive narrative in contemporary popular culture. Film is part of the text of everyday life that teaches the nexus of sexual violence. The "war narrative" is comprised of a private, internal movie, a shared personal narrative, and a public, cultural icon, the war movie. "War movie" encompasses more than films that explicitly take war as their subject, however. Seen in the context of this nexus of sexual and political violence, many visual texts invoke and reinforce the coercive power of a culture of sexual terror by coupling the subjects of gender war and political authority. Such texts often transmit the dual message of an ungovernable gender war, "controlled" by law and order—a message of powerlessness that contributes to despair and the desire for absolute authority. The power of such tales can be analyzed from three perspectives; the internal movie, the shared narration, and the cultural icon. The concept of the "gaze," used in contemporary film theory, applies in each of these loci of meaning.

Film theorists use the concept of the gaze to analyze the sources of power embodied in the visual image. The gaze establishes a relationship of authority between subject and object, dominated through the gaze. To gaze is to control or possess, or to objectify others, "subjecting them to a controlling and curious gaze."[5]

Film critics can find this authority in three viewpoints: the camera's perspective, the look on screen, and the gaze of the audience or spectator. Each of these perspectives exerts power over the action and meaning of a text, either by overtly controlling perspective through *mise-en-scene* (the placing of action into the scene), or by signaling subject and object positions through symbolic text. The gender differences in the gaze are characterized by Mulvey and others as a triad of camera, man on screen, and male spectator (or, less frequently, the female spectator who has been invited to identify with the male gaze as an objectified female). This triad appears to mirror the gendered nature of power in society.[6] The camera constructs a text in which the male subject manipulates means and meaning in action and reinforces the male spectator's beliefs about the object acted upon.

THEORETICAL LINKS BETWEEN SEXUAL AND POLITICAL VIOLENCE

The saying "May the force be with you," from the popular film *Star Wars* presents a perplexing, if not contradictory, twist to a greeting intending goodwill and protection. It at once recognizes the need for force in one's life and conjures the idea that if armed with "the force," one could defend, compel, and control oneself and others. Through the use of "the force," one could "do unto others" for the good of all—so that good would prevail.

In this imagined, future world, we are presented with a clear distinction between good and evil, between justified "good" force and evil "bad" force. The characters in *Star Wars* give a clear representation of evil in the faceless Darth Vader of the Evil Empire, clothed in black, doing battle with the young, vibrant all-American Luke Skywalker, who represents good force. The greeting gained immediate, widespread currency because we have internalized the concept of just or good force and have given our assent to physical force as a protection against illegitimate force and violence.

The concept of a good force, a commonplace in liberal political theory, maintains that coercive power enforces all rule-ordered relationships. Most political analysts accept the necessity of force and the view that authority is founded on the threat and use of force against law breakers. Legitimate force, though not often a conscious concern for the law-abiding person, conditions everyday reality.

Although the world of laser beams and starships promotes an impression of its innocuous quality, legitimate force is not so simply benign and is, itself, subject to rules. Self-government requires a regulated sort of freedom. In democracy, authority is designed for structured opposition—all authority is to be limited in a self-governing system.[7] The mature political judgment required for a self-governing citizenry includes the capacity to evaluate legitimate and illegitimate uses of force. Citizens must be able to discern methods of coercion that are not only illegitimate, but may control through covert channels of intimidation. Sexual violence, as feminist theory suggests, may be one such illegitimate, covert, coercive tool, employing terror as a means of control. In this case, private terror, rather than public terrorism, transmits the message of authority.

Gender dominance amounts to more than unequal pay and segregated political participation. Ideologies of domination reduce our capacity to govern ourselves by reflection and choice, instead of fate and force. Believing that some human beings should, by nature, be dominated through violent force by others, restricts our account of humanity's self-governing capacity. In the case of gender dominance, we are not only less able to think critically about legitimate and illegitimate uses of force, we may even justify the use of sexual violence to establish political rule. Force as political violence is observed and experienced in warfare, terrorism, and torture. Force as cultural violence is observed and experienced in rape and sexual terror. If, as feminist theorists argue, gender dominance is the basis for political rule, those who cannot dominate sexually cannot rule.

EXPLORING GENDER DOMINANCE AND
POLITICAL RULE THROUGH FILM

Film texts provide an important arena in which to observe the conjunction of private and public authority and are important to the study of politics for at least three reasons. First, as a part of popular culture, film reflects the ways we think about relationships of power, including legitimate political authority and coercion occurring outside the sphere of government. Second, as a powerful means of socialization, film instructs us, influencing how we understand the forces that structure authority in liberal societies, the permeable boundaries of public and private, the relationship of democratic citizens to government, and the relationship between the threat or exercise of force in one sphere and coercion in the other. Third, as an art form, film gives authors and interpreters of texts a medium through which assumptions about our world, including authority relationships, may be explored. The language of film reflects an authoritative narrative that reproduces itself in private texts of power, revealing, recreating, and reinforcing an understanding of authority at odds with the consciousness required for self government. As an important cultural icon, film mirrors the lessons of sexual politics that Kate Millett uncovers in the text of real life.

In 1920, a group of artists developed techniques to explore our unconscious repository of basic responses to authority. The writers and visual artists of the surrealist movement used sexual metaphors as a vehicle for challenging generally accepted ideas about political authority. Louis Bunuel's surrealist film *Un Chien Andalou* (Andalousian Dog) exemplifies this avant-garde exploration. One half century later, Lina Wertmuller explored the nexus of political and sexual domination in her films *Swept Away* and *Summer Nights*. Her work uses sexual domination as a metaphor of political terrorism, revolution, and legitimate rule. Presenting the protagonists' sexual encounters as metaphors for political struggles in modern-day Italian politics, her work not only helps us examine questions related to political authority, but, more fundamentally, raises questions about the use of sexual domination for political rule. The work of these artists suggests an inseparable nexus of sexual dominance and political violence in all designs of political authority.

The television series "Twin Peaks" demonstrates the cliché popular culture has made of sexual assault, incest, and murder in a small town. This modern fusion of politics and sexual violence not only contributes to cultural numbness to sexual violence but also imparts a general indifference to political authority. As an imitation of the surrealist genre, "Twin Peaks" couples dependence on paternalistic political authority with defense of sexual terror as the unremarkable evil that men do.

Comparing the 1961 film *Cape Fear*, with its 1991 re-make shows the extent to which sexual violence is now commonplace and the duplicitous message of law and licentiousness that is liberal patriarchy's staple. Both versions of the film explore the tension between political and patriarchal authority. The characters find themselves capitulating to alternative desires for absolute rule or a state of nature in order to control ungovernable sexual violence.

THE FILMS: DISCUSSION AND ANALYSIS

A classic example of Surrealism from the 1920s, the film *Un Chien Andalou* provides material for a discussion of the metaphorical use of women's bodies in an artistic practice with a political purpose. This film exemplifies the surrealists' use of symbolic visual language including eroticized metaphor to engage the viewer's unconscious in transgressing consensually held belief and our general acquiescence to authority.[8] *Un Chien Andalou* uses sexual violence to explore cultural and political authority, demonstrating a better understanding of the surrealists' purposes.

Surrealism's Purpose and Technique

The surrealists' artistic practice proposed to "effect radical change and innovation *both* in the symbolic field *and* in the social and political realm of everyday life."[9] These practices, consisting of techniques that motivated the spectator to view texts in a new way, even questioned the perception of text as a unitary, readable, and intelligible whole.[10] The surrealists related the artistic text to daily life, which was itself conceived as a text. They linked artistic practice to political practice, arguing that all activity could be understood as text, and all authority for creating and interpreting these texts could be questioned through the "disruption" of text.

The surrealists accomplished this disruption of text through techniques of discontinuity, "sliding," heterogeneity or collage, rupture, linguistic transformation, repetition, and symbolic inversion. Disruption of the text amounted to nothing less than a disruption of consciousness, including our reliance on symbolic logic, especially linguistic practice, and the authority of reason—essentially all the foundational elements for constructing a conscious reality.

Un Chien Andalou

Luis Bunuel's and Salvador Dali's 1928 film *Un Chien Andalou* is a classic example of surrealist use of woman as cypher and the use of techniques that employ politically motivated, self-conscious, symbolic violence to transgress political authority. *Un Chien Andalou* moves the viewer through a series of metaphors, attempting to destroy sense and dissolve it into psychoanalytic clichés. The film can be read as a deconstruction of Freudian construction of the conscious.[11]

The prologue of *Un Chien Andalou* uses violence as a vehicle to rupture the text of culture, setting up a preposterous similarity between the cutting of a woman's eye by a razor and the cutting of the moon by the horizontal sliver of a cloud. In her brilliantly detailed analysis of the film, Linda Williams points out how the moon/cloud and eye/razor sequence disrupts the usual hierarchy of metaphoric vehicle in which the thing that the object is like is usually secondary, or in the background, and the object itself is placed in the text as primary, or as foreground material.[12] In this case, the figural or vehicle half of the metaphor comes first and appears to generate the action that follows. The figure deconstructs the metaphoric process, and the metaphor "the cloud slices the moon" (which, as Williams points out, is already a figure of speech) now becomes the action of the scene, with the violent cutting of the eye becoming the metaphor. As Williams explains, "This metaphoric act of violence . . . unlike most film violence, subverts the realism of its discourse."[13] This physical violence, Williams argues, cues the textual violence. She suggests that the cutting that follows is nothing less than the implementation of the meta-metaphor, "the ironic symbol of the hand of the artist at work cutting up the continuous fabric of 'reality' into newly significant combinations."[14] The inversion of the usual hierarchy of metaphor calls into question all that follows—including the search for meaning. Because of the enigmatic prologue, we are asked to suspend the process of interpretation and see the film. The prologue, Williams argues, opens the eye to see.

Lina Wertmuller's Use of Sexual Violence as Metaphor for Political Revolution

Films of another narrative style allow viewers to see more deeply into the use of sexual violence as a vehicle for exploring political violence. Lina Wertmuller's *Swept Away* and *Summer Nights* explore the relationship of sexual dominance to political rule. Wertmuller explores the nature of political authority through the language of film. Her narratives integrate the personal authority conferred by society's economic, class, gender, and race-based power with political authority. She looks explicitly at the link between personal power exercised in the private sphere and political power expressed in public relationships. She particularly explores contests between capitalism and socialism, environmentalists and industrialists, terrorists and ruling elites, men and women, the rich and working class, and the white aristocracy and a dark-skinned ethnic worker in Italy.

In her 1975 film *Swept Away to an Unusual Destiny in the Blue Sea of August*, Raffaella (Mariangela Melato), the fair, female, Milanese plutocrat, represents bourgeois capitalism's fixation on ostentatious displays of wealth and consequent power as well as its hypocritical paternal attitude toward the working class. In contrast, Gennarino (Giancarlo Gianini), the dark-skinned, male, Sicilian proletarian, representing social revolt and the simple life, ultimately masters her heart and soul when the plot takes them from Raffaella's luxury yacht in the Mediterranean and leaves them stranded on a deserted island.

This film not only presents a critique of capitalism and socialist strategies of revolt but also presents a complex analysis of gendered power relationships and a subtle exploration of white skin privilege and cultural constructions of race. The viewer is asked to analyze the locus of power for each character. Raffaella appears to have no power without her economic and social class status, a depiction applicable to the text of real life. The only apparent choice for Gennarino is to enter into a revolutionary struggle that he can win only in terms of physical and sexual domination. The prior state of Raffaella's domination by economic means is overthrown, the roles are reversed, and the underlying patriarchal structure of dominance through rape rises to power. The possibility for creating a relationship between the two characters based on the principle of equal authority seems nonexistent (although their desert environment would not seem to preclude their inventing a nonhierarchical relationship for themselves). Wertmuller uses sexual violence to emphasize the probability that merely overthrowing the ruling class, only to replace the old guard with a few new faces (while maintaining the same authority design), will result in nothing more than a failed revolt.

In an especially provocative turn of the plot, Wertmuller uses Raffaella's literal rape to symbolize the politics of failed revolution. Through the rape, Gennarino becomes her master, and rape becomes the medium for expressing his authority. This scene provides the foundation for a political analysis of the intersection of race, gender, and class politics. By depicting their fundamental relationship (sans social constructions of class and capitalist power) as one of hostility, Wertmuller provides numerous examples for discussing Kate Millett's argument that the political follows from the personal. The sexual violence can be analyzed as political violence within the framework of patriarchal politics and in the film's concern with a symbolic presentation of social revolt.

In *Summer Nights with Greek Profile, Almond Eyes and Scent of Basil* (1986), Wertmuller attempts to confront critics who charged her with sexism and misogyny in *Swept Away*. Squarely facing those who were outraged that a woman signified capitalism and her rape the allegorical equivalent for failed revolt, Wertmuller transforms the gendered situation in *Summer Nights*. In this film it is the woman (Mariangela Melato) who holds a young terrorist (Michele Placido) captive, raising questions about gender privilege, a woman's potential for perpetrating sexual terror, and the relationship of political and economic power to sexual domination.

The film presents the story of a revolutionary young man who leads a terrorist band that kidnaps members of the ruling class and ransoms them for millions. The female protagonist, a rich, environmentally chic industrialist, tires of this constant threat to her cohort. With the voice of an enlightened capitalist (who makes money by zealously protecting the environment), she explains that the rich are responsible for Italy's greatness. Meeting with her peers, she raises money to hire her own terrorist, an assassin and architect of covert political revelries. Along with the droll depiction of the female protagonist, the absurd characterization of the assassin as a victim of a number of failed plots or "field accidents" that have left him without an eye, hand, and foot, creates the farcical context for the film's sexual adventure as political skirmish. The hired assassin kidnaps the kidnapper and delivers him to the woman for ransom to his terrorist ring.

The film opens with the capture of this beautiful young terrorist from his merry band's picturesque hideout on a Mediterranean beach. Brought to a white dungeon at one of the woman's palatial island estates, he is chained like an animal and responds with primal charm, including animal magnetism and sexuality. Leaving him for a month in the hands of her hired kidnappers, the woman departs to rendezvous with her Swedish lover, a rather tame member of Europe's ruling class. Although she dominates this relationship, her unbridled nature (left unnoticed by her lover) sets her on a personal quest to explore the untamed.

Before departing, she announces whimsically that her prisoner be given only bread and water—a torture she seems to have in her vocabulary from fiction. Taking this order literally, her hired kidnappers nearly destroy the beautiful boy terrorist. Upon returning she orders him restored to health. Placing him unshackled, but blindfolded in paradise, she revives him with caviar and champagne. In a witty, sarcastic turn, Wertmuller has her female protagonist contemplate the youth's spiritual admonishment to examine the excesses of her own life. As a fanatical environmentalist, she is only too ready to undertake this challenge, within acceptable boundaries of asceticism: wine and paté replace champagne and caviar.

Revived, the boy terrorist asks that other deprivations be alleviated, lest he suffer the cruel and unusual punishment of sexual abstinence. Conjugal rights appertain to any man, married or not, he argues; he "services" his prisoners, especially women, and expects such civil treatment from his captor. In response to this request, she argues with him about Italian politics.

She discusses obtaining prostitutes for her prisoner with her hired guns, who vehemently disagree with her and believe he should be tortured if they are to obtain restitution for the rich Italians he has kidnapped. They fear that if he enjoys captivity he not only will refuse to authorize ransom, he may want to remain captive. As a male concern, this indicates that what women may experience as sexual violence at the hands of their male captors may be experienced by men in the same situation as sexual pleasure. Throughout these deliberations, the hired assassin, subdued by his employer's power, is falling in love with this "bitch who breaks [his] balls."

Her entrepreneurial style encompasses the management of all the men in the drama. Applying her skills to the task of kidnapping the kidnapper, she embraces patriarchal behaviors usually attributable to men, minus the threat of sexual violence. She uses her money, intelligence, and beauty to exercise control; yet her recognition of the need for force leads her to employ men who are capable of using it. Controlling the altercation with her assassin, she hires two beautiful prostitutes, who are elated with the prospect of having sex with this sensuous captured terrorist. With an opportunity to explore the untamed, the woman joins the two prostitutes for the sexual encounter. Discerning his captor's presence, he wants only her, and without admitting her identity to the blindfolded youth, she obliges. He subdues her sexually, but she enjoys the encounter on her own terms as well. When his colleagues agree to pay his ransom, she is willing to release him. As a true capitalist, her intent was never to destroy her captive, but to get the money.

Triumphant, she returns to a fete her rich peers vaunt to celebrate her coup. Manipulating her cohort as she has everyone else, she manages to keep most of the ransom. In the film's finale, the tables turn, and, along with her assassin, she is captured and delivered to her terrorist-lover on the beach of his Mediterranean hideout. In the next scene, we see her with her captor on his horse, unbound, gleefully riding off into the sunset. In a last farcical moment they fall, laughing, from his horse. Fitting with the film's tone, the light ending makes kidnapping, bondage, and sexual service look like fun; potential terror turns to farce.

In *Summer Nights*, women are in charge of their own sexuality and control their own destiny, including their sexual destiny. Unlike in *Swept Away*, these women do not depend on dominating men to meet their needs; women can dominate. These films raise important questions about whether women can dominate men sexually, without personal expense. Wertmuller's work suggests that if women cannot dominate sexually, they cannot truly dominate politically.

"Twin Peaks" and Surrealism

My students introduced me to "Twin Peaks" midway through the series. They were captivated by the avant-garde techniques used by coproducers

David Lynch and Mark Frost. In several respects, Lynch and Frost may be seen as offering much less than a new way of seeing and much less than a vanguard view of cultural and political reality. Given the current effect of feminist criticism on deconstruction—a contemporary manifestation of many surrealist concerns—an avant-garde project might well be expected to concern itself with the rupture of the male gaze.[15] Lynch and Frost, on the contrary, embrace the male subject position, disrupting nothing of the socio-political text. Far from offering a new vision, by assigning culpability for in-cest to the Devil, Lynch and Frost construct the plot with a reality attuned to a romantic, religious worldview—one against which surrealists paraded their parodies. Popular use of surrealist techniques in such contemporary cultural icons as "Twin Peaks" or music video, appear largely to abandon the political nature of the avant-garde project and demonstrate Adorno and Horkheimer's perception that the culture industry can degrade political dis-course to cliché.[16]

"Twin Peaks" first aired as a miniseries on ABC in the spring of 1989, its noir starting point being the murder of high school homecoming queen Laura Palmer and the brutal assault on her classmate Ronette Pulaski. Called in to take charge of the murder investigation is Agent Dale Cooper, a curious mix of a stereotypically uptight FBI agent and New Age eccentric. Agent Cooper exhibits a penchant for hanging from rafters by his heels with gravity boots, talking passionately about the Dalai Lama's exodus to Tibet in 1959, and depending on strange dreams for clues to the murder.

College campuses, television critics, and intellectuals enthusiastically received "Twin Peaks" as an avant-garde television show, an understanding that was enhanced by the reputations of its coproducers, filmmaker David Lynch (of *Blue Velvet* and *Elephant Man* fame) and television director Mark Frost (of "Hill Street Blues" fame). Achieving almost instant cult status, "Twin Peaks" gained high ratings among 18- to 49-year-olds[17] and inspired devoted fans to form clubs and host parties, gathering in groups to watch the show and consume the coffee, doughnuts, and cherry pie that were favorites of Cooper and "Twin Peaks" sheriff Harry S. Truman.[18]

Many TV critics were also enthusiastic about the show, particularly its early episodes. Media sociologist Todd Gitlin described "Twin Peaks" as the first "prime time postmodern television series produced by a major net-work."[19] A writer for *City Pages*, a news and arts weekly in Minneapolis and St. Paul, Minnesota, described it as "the most exciting thing to ever hit American TV."[20] One critic for *The Nation* called "Twin Peaks" subversive "in a medium largely devoted to 'delivering' demographic numbers to ad-vertisers with formulaic programming."

Culturally, *Twin Peaks* is the dark side of the myth of small-town decency, a myth Ronald Reagan cultivated and traduced. Sociologically, it is the Lynds' Middletown updated to post-Reagan America; unhappy marriages, violence against women, pervasive drugs, merchandised sex, failing industry. (At the center of the plot is the sale of the sawmill to foreign developers by the town's Michael Milken.) There's a dark evil out in those woods and only F.B.I. agent Dale Cooper and sheriff Harry S. Truman can save us. Cooper, the last young conservative innocent, came to town still believing in the small-town dream, but in *Twin Peaks* he discovered the nightmare.[21]

National Review, assured readers that David Lynch was not "your basic left-wing *avant-garde* muckraker of the national soul," but some authors were less sanguine about this mix of avant-garde and conservative politics. "Twin Peaks's" appropriation of surrealist techniques replicated the political rhetoric of Ronald Reagan's mythic America.[22] The former president conjured a blissful "morning in America," which was in marked contrast with his rhetoric eliciting images of America facing the earlier mentioned "Evil Empire" of *Star Wars* and the next administration's more explicit exhortation to a nation preyed upon by "Willie Hortons" who rupture small town life. Reagan's rhetoric provided an interesting construction for determining reality, one that suggested that we shape reality to reflect art, or, in this case, to represent fiction—a reversal from the normally held belief that art expresses an artist's view of reality.

The murderer in "Twin Peaks" was not a Willie Horton free on parole, however, but Laura Palmer's father, possessed by an evil demon named Bob. Although director David Lynch claimed to be exploring the seamy side, the "ooze" of the small town, viewers are not enlightened by this portrayal of humanity's evil side. The reality of sexual violence has indelibly ruptured the textual consciousness for many, and attributing culpability to phantoms does little to transgress the text of the status quo.

A look at how "Twin Peaks" represents authority gives us more evidence that the series reinforces the prevailing understanding of political rule, rather than offering serious ideas about responsibility for safety and freedom in the private and public spheres. The series portrayed the gendered authority of a patriarchy that relies on a culture of sexual terror for maintaining its political authority that in turn supports a rape culture. In the world of "Twin Peaks" only the police and the FBI represent moral order—by bringing not humans to justice but specters to an exorcism.

The myth of phallic potency forms the symbolic subtext for the series overt action as the solution to Laura's murder unfolds. This myth lives even in the wheelchair-bound "Twin Peaks" character Leo Johnson, a drug-dealing truck driver who remains a physical threat to his wife even after he is critically wounded and becomes a quadriplegic. Johnson retains his threatening demeanor during a memorable birthday party—the epitome of childhood celebration. Although catatonic, drooling, and wearing a party hat while sitting in his wheelchair in front of a cake, he is still able to threaten and control his wife through the intensity of his gaze upon her.

In contrast to the paradigm of phallic potency illustrated in mythic proportions by this quadriplegic male, female characters in the show (from recollections of Laura to the reinvention of entreprenuese Catherine Martell as a powerful Japanese businessman) lack power in any sphere. This text of victimization is epitomized in Nadine Hurely, who awakens from a coma with superhuman strength, but is rendered harmless because she believes she is an 18–year-old perpetually preparing to try out for the high school cheerleader squad. One of the only women not living under the threat of physical harm in "Twin Peaks" is Log Lady, a character who limits most of her socializing to a phallic log, which offers her wisdom and perhaps protection.

In addition to the subterranean ideation of phallic potency, even "Twin Peaks's" superficial depictions of women evinces this cooperation with gender stereotypes and sexism. Besides standing for the mountains of the Pacific Northwest, the peaks in "Twin Peaks" simultaneously serve as a euphemism for women's breasts—a fact admitted by co-producer Mark Frost[23] and recognized by male admirers, including a writer for *Rolling Stone*, who described his interview with three of the female stars as a chat with six of the "many twin peaks" appearing in the series.[24] "Twin Peaks" contributed to cultural attitudes about sexual violence in more harmful ways than merely its title's sexist symbolism and the objectifying of women's bodies. "Twin Peaks" is a place where women live with the constant threat of violence from men, the sexual terror on which patriarchal authority relies. Linked to the series's obvious sexism, sexual violence becomes a topic of humor instead of a terror to be treated seriously. More than simply looking at sexist treatment of male and female characters, feminist critics of gender difference in film link "a privileging of vision with a sexual privilege,"[25] exposing a dynamic of power that is more harmful than the simple sophomoric sexist tone of the series. The concept of the gaze establishes this relationship between vision and sexual privilege. As a result, viewers are taught to understand only one conception of authority—paternalistic power and control of women by men. More critical appraisals of authority are impossible when the basic construction of objectifying and appropriating women as "others" remains unexamined.

To the extent that a gendered gaze persists, the project of disrupting the ongoing cultural text of authority is jeopardized. Even when surrealist techniques are founded on radical politics, the male gaze undercuts the use of sexual violence to probe political authority. In "Twin Peaks," the power of the gaze in the author's presentation demonstrates the reactionary nature of this text.

"Twin Peaks" is presented as an exploration of the universal themes of good and evil, innocence and guilt. However, the central text of incest and physical violence against women is left largely unexplored in terms of its own politics and in terms of its ramifications for politics in the world beyond television text, the text of reality. Lynch's singular lack of insight into the text of incest contrasts with the prologue to the surrealist film *Un Chien Andalou* that it parodies. The reference made to the surrealist film precedes the series's second murder and rape revealing the solution to the six-month-long mystery: the perpetrator of the crime against Laura is none other than her father, Leland. The entire sequence of the murder and rape of Maddy, Laura's cousin, follows much of the farcical exploration of sexual assault in the Dali and Bunuel film. However, in the case of "Twin Peaks," the clouds bisect the moon, revealing nothing but the utter lack of human responsibility for evil. The episode that closes the case on Laura's murder shows a dying Leland, killed by the devil, Bob, who has caused him to kill and rape his daughter. He explains his predicament to himself: "I killed her. I killed my daughter." Continuing, he explains his possession by the demonic Bob:

I was just a boy. I saw him in my dream. He asked me if I wanted to play. He offered me and I invited him and he came inside me. When he was inside I didn't know and when he was gone I couldn't remember. He made me do things, terrible things. I was just a boy. I saw him in my dream. He asked me if I wanted to play. He offered me and I invited him and he came inside me. When he was inside I didn't know and when he was gone I couldn't remember. He made me do things, terrible things.[26]

Laura's experience as a teenager, sexually abused by her father/Bob, parallels the pathology of how incest is handled in many families—through denial and silence, with Laura's mother refusing to acknowledge the sexual violence occurring under the roof of the family home. During the rape and murder of Maddy, Laura's cousin, the mother lies in a catatonic stupor at the edge of the action.

A plot that locates evil outside social and political structures is believable only when we accept a construction of gender roles complicit with patriarchy's rape culture. Placing responsibility for violence in evilness, nature, or other metaphysical causes is necessary only as a means of alleviating men of their responsibility for violence against women. In solving Laura Palmer's murder in the segment's closing scene, Sheriff Harry S. Truman observes: "There's a sort of evil out there. Something very very strange in these old woods. Call it what you want, a darkness, a presence; it takes many forms and it's been out there as long as anyone can remember and we always have been here to fight it."27

After the mystery is solved, Agent Cooper, Sheriff Truman and FBI forensics expert Albert Rosenfield provide what becomes the show's explanation of Leland/Bob's rampage of abuse and murder.

"He was completely insane," offers Truman.

"People saw him in visions," counters Rosenfield, who finds it hard to accept psychosis as the cause of Leland's actions. Adds Truman: "I've seen some strange things but this is way off the map. I'm having a hard time believing."

Cooper then adds his piece. "Harry, is it easier to believe a man would rape and murder his own daughter?" The episode ends as Rosenfield speculates that Bob is "the evil that men do."28

SEXUAL TERROR AND LAW: CAPE FEAR IN 1961 AND 1991

Cape Fear tangibly relates sexual violence to political authority by exploring the American legal system's treatment of rape and battery. Both versions of the film raise complex questions about stalking, rape, the victimization of victims, culpability of adolescents, and the control of women through sexual terror. The films' characterizations and action accurately reflect changes in the treatment of sexual violence between the original 1962 film and Martin Scorsese's remake in 1991. Both films, however, present the same essential plot.

Max Cady (Robert Mitchem/Robert De Niro) imprisoned for a brutal sexual assault (seven years in the 1961 version, fourteen years in the 1991 film), returns to a small southern town to stalk and harass the wife and daughter of the lawyer responsible for his imprisonment. In the original version, lawyer Sam Bowden (Gregory Peck) witnessed the assault while on a business trip and provided key testimony to convict Cady. In Scorsese's film, Sam (Nick Nolte), acting as Cady's defense attorney, takes the law into his own hands and suppresses information about the assaulted teenager's past "promiscuity." His failure to provide an adequate defense of his client contributes to Cady's conviction. In 1961, Sam, the good citizen, is innocent of any wrongdoing; in 1991, Sam, acting against his constitutional duty, uses his information and authority to convict Cady, rather than defend him.

Neither man is innocent in 1991. Sam, who is himself guilty of a crime, experiences his own kind of terror at the hands of Cady, that of being discovered and possibly disbarred. Cady, who intends to "teach Sam about loss," is depicted as a religious fanatic, a medium of the wrath of God, punishing sexual transgressions such as promiscuity, as well as Sam's betrayal as his attorney fourteen years earlier. In this personal declared war, Cady intends to feminize Sam, the loser (bring him to his knees so to speak), by using Sam's daughter, Danielle's, body as the medium for "doing battle" and teaching the lesson (Danielle is played by Lori Marton in 1961 and Juliette Lewis in 1991). His harassment of the family portends the intended rape of the daughter.

In the 30 years between the issuing of these films, society had witnessed dramatic change in cultural attitudes about sex and violence. The portrayal of sexual violence and violence in these films reflects these changes in law and culture. Viewing both versions reveals startling change in family life, particularly concerning the responses of different members to sex, violence, and sexual terror, with some differences in the focus of the films' male gaze.

In the Scorsese film, violence is integral to Danielle's sexual development. Violence permeates the film and her environment. Most of the violence is sexualized (MTV is used as a background cypher of the nexus of sex and violence), and violence is prevalent in most family scenes and in other intimate contexts (her parents fight openly about their sexual relationship and marital fidelity). Danielle is a captive audience for her parents' marital disputes, she is aware that her father is a guilt-ridden sexual addict, MTV dispenses a constant barrage of visual sexual assault, and Henry Miller's *Sexus* is her bedtime reading. The film's dialogue focuses on sexual imagery and the conjunction of sex and violence from the initial close-up of Max Cady's "girly" cigarette lighter through the constant background of violent cultural icons to the explicit sexual terror of the film's denouement.

Sexual violence, sexual taboo, and sexual transgressions are treated ambiguously in 1991. Following the opening melange of male gaze that concludes with the objectified female body as cigarette lighter, Sam and his wife, Leigh (Jessica Lange), discuss Danielle's expulsion from school for smoking marijuana. In rambling dialogue, Sam offers his opinion about the school's overzealous reaction. Leigh, in a nearly inaudible response, sarcastically links this infraction with sexual taboo. Standing in the background she says: "It's right up there with incest, necrophilia, and bestiality." Not only are these sexual transgressions dismissed by the inappropriate equation drawn between them and the misdemeanor of marijuana use, but a similarity is drawn between sexual taboo and sexual violence, exemplifying the film's ambivalence about the difference between sex and violence.

In the original version, there is nothing ambiguous about these characters' guilt or innocence, the wickedness of violence, and Max Cady's depravity.

Nor are sex and violence confused in 1961—as demonstrated by the different kinds of warnings given by the men of the house to their women. The original *Cape Fear* portrays Max Cady's threat as a violent, not a sexual act. In 1961, violence, rather than sex, is the focus of Sam's warning to the women. Treating his wife and daughter as equals under male protection, Sam speaks to both as his wife intently listens and watches for her daughter's reactions.

Sam: I'd like to speak to both of you. I'm not telling you this to frighten you, but I want you to be careful and I think you're old enough to be told why. Eight years ago I was a witness against a man. And he was sent to prison, and the thing is he's out now and blames me for his conviction.

Danielle: He's the one that poisoned Marilyn [the family's dog].

Sam: Maybe, but we have no proof of that.

Danielle: But you know he did.

Sam: Thinking isn't knowing. Just be careful. This is a big man, he smokes cigars and wears a panama hat, I'll get you a police photo. Until we have this under control I want you to never leave this house or grounds except in your mother's car. There's nothing to worry about as long as you are careful. The police are keeping a very close watch on the house and chances are he's just trying to scare us anyway.

Sam projects the calm belief that law and order will prevail and protect the family. Only later is his faith in law shaken. Although Sam appears to view his wife as needing protection, not unlike his child, subsequent scenes show wife and husband are each capable of critical appraisal of their circumstances. They work together to devise a scheme of protection. Each also deters the other from impulsive behavior that could lead to tragedy.

The 1991 version brings ambiguous moral standards for sex, violence, and legal transgression. Sam's anxiety results less from sexual terror than from misgivings and the fear of punishment for his own wrongdoings. Sam fears the direct harm of exposure and disbarment more than Cady's threat of an indirect attack through the women of his household. Because Sam's agenda of control and concealment is complicated by his own immorality, neither wife nor daughter ever hear the complete story from him. This lack of information increases his power and control over them and maintains the relationship of male domination.

The first conversation between Sam and Leigh takes place in the kitchen. She asks Sam why Cady was in prison, and he skillfully evades her question with a partial truth, "I think for battery." She presses him, "Well, who did he batter, did he batter a man, did he batter a woman?" He pretends a memory lapse, "I really don't know, it was 14 years ago." Sam's concerns revolve around his own ethical lapse, his misrepresentation as Cady's defense attorney, marital infidelity, and a spouse who has never completely recovered from a serious depression. Culpability for sexual violence is difficult to assign in a world without moral firmament—one in which all transgressions are equally ambiguous.

Sam first warns Leigh about Cady nonchalantly, running out the door for work, "I don't want to alarm her [Danielle] but I'd rather she not wander out alone." "Just tell her" he snaps. "Tell her what? I hardly know anything," Leigh responds. He continues to rush out the door replying, "I don't mean his biography, just that there is some creep around." He then adds this afterthought, "If you see anything call the cops and then call me."

Only later does Leigh learn the nature of Cady's crime. Turning to walk out of a room, upset by a phone call about Cady, Sam mumbles: "He raped another girl." In astonishment Leigh exclaims, "Raped! I thought you said battery!" Although all of this adult discussion seems to take place within earshot of Danielle, her presence and the threat of real danger for her safety seem barely acknowledged. A direct threat to her safety is another instance of background violence in the text of her life. The argument that ensues is only one of the many constant arguments between her parents in which sex is subtext. She consequently gives this bit of subtext no more credence than she gives the staple of violence already permeating her environment.

Sam's control of information leaves his wife and daughter vulnerable and subsequently unable to make choices about their own safety. His warnings to his daughter are given in a clumsy way, but they nonetheless clearly assert his control. In the process, he belittles, embarrasses, shames, and confuses her further about which man is good, which evil.

Sam's anxiety about his daughter's unwillingness to see Cady's evilness and his attempts to control her increase with every scene. Believing that Danielle's sexual development increases her vulnerability to Cady's violence (subsequently increasing his own vulnerability), he escalates his attempts to control her physically and emotionally. This desire for control not only reflects cultural assumptions about the causes and culpability for sexual violence, it betrays Sam's ambivalent relationship to his daughter's sexual development. Sam's objectifying gaze is often directed at his daughter's body, conveying to her that she is not only a temptation to him and a pawn to Cady's dementia, but that her sexual development is the primary cause of her vulnerability. In response to his guilt about his inappropriate reaction to her body, he attacks her, leaving her bewildered and angry. Sam enters his daughter's bedroom, believing she has had an encounter with Cady. Danielle, lying on her bed in her underwear, listens to her father's speech about staying away from Cady. He turns to leave her room saying with a judging scowl, "and put some clothes on, you're not a little kid anymore." She counters, taunting him defiantly, "Dad, he didn't force himself on me you know. I know you'd like to think that he did, but he was just trying to make a connection." Sam's reaction to this disclosure results in a physically violent move to cover up her mouth, as if he couldn't bear to hear another word.

Sam's philandering and inability to deal appropriately with his daughter's development is placed on par with Cady's violence against women. Sam behaves within the parameters of patriarchy analyzed by Millett. Yet Sam, while behaving as a patriarch, is not a rapist. This foundational ambiguity and equation invites us to understand sexual abuse as part of a continuum of control and dominance within sexual politics. The role of the film's male gaze confuses this portion of the analysis, however. Although Danielle's prologue and epilogue frame the story in 1991, this is less her story than that of the dominant gaze upon her. She is placed before the camera as a mix of nubile temptation. The gaze upon her constructs her as the focus of action, as an object of male manipulation—Cady's and her father's.

The daughters differ significantly in the two versions, resulting in different explorations of adolescent sexuality and father/daughter, mother/daughter relationships. In the 1991 version, this pubescent adolescent, recently expelled from high school for smoking marijuana, is not as innocent as the daughter in 1961. In one scene, the mother, trying to make being held captive in your own home a pleasant moment for mother and daughter to spend time together, is confronted by her daughter with: "Is it because he was a flasher or just a peeper?" "How do you know about that?" responds the mother. "Don't you think I've been flashed before?" says Danielle. "Oh, I certainly didn't mean to insult you, I'm sure you've been flashed before," says her mother sarcastically.

In fact, in 1991, Max Cady, using the daughter's adolescent fight against authority, her confusion about her own sexual awakenings, and her alienation from a philandering father and emotionally unbalanced mother, seduces her. Posing as her drama teacher, Cady calls her one night for a sympathetic chat that validates her rebellion against her parents, using this entree to arrange a rendezvous during school the next day (an interaction that calls into question appropriate adult-teen relationships). She is clearly attracted to Cady's sexual innuendo and his "hip" adult act and apparent understanding of her rebellion against very stodgy parents. He asks if she would mind if he put his arm around her. After a bashful and embarrassing look, she says, "No, I don't mind." The scene that follows shows the daughter in a coy, yet almost innocent way, sucking Cady's finger and then succumbing to his advance to kiss her. Caught between childhood and adolescence, she initially is enthralled by what is happening to her, then turns and runs away frightened.

So ambiguous are these perceptions of her father and Max Cady, that the daughter cannot imagine that her father is right and Cady is a bad man. Abandoned in a moral haze, she must make her own judgments, and regardless of how sophisticated she may appear, she is missing the tools for discriminating between good and bad. In 1961 the rules were clearer and children could count on their parents to protect them and help them learn the difference between good and bad. In 1991, it is not until Danielle witnesses the results of Cady's wrath—the murder of a hired detective and the housekeeper—that she begins to heed her parents' warnings.

In 1961, although the fashions of the day included tight bodices and short shorts, the daughter seems oblivious to her sexuality and the threat of rape. She is defiantly less "street-wise" than her counterpart in 1991, yet displays an attitude of maturity and comfort with herself that is missing in the 1991 Danielle.

Both films view rape as an act of one man against the property of another, in this case the property of a man's family, his wife and daughter. Both explore dilemma posed for a justice system that values the innocence of the accused and demands the testimony of the victim in determinations at trial. These films explore the reasons why women often do not testify against a rapist. In both *Cape Fear* renditions the view of the justice system remains stable. Both films understand that victims of sexual violence will be victimized a second time in a court of law.

In each film, Max Cady procures a woman and brutally rapes her. Terrified by his savagery, both characters refuse to be used by Sam to testify against Cady—an act that would potentially save Sam's family. The victim in 1961 explains, "Do you believe that I could ever in my whole life step up to another living soul and repeat what this man, what he did?" In the 1991 film, this attack includes cannibalism; yet fear alone does not prevent the women from testifying. In 1991, the victim, a law clerk, is acutely aware of how rape victims are treated in court. She fears the humiliation of hearing her past displayed as promiscuous—whether or not this be a just interpretation. She knows her coworkers in the justice system snicker about the rape victims they encounter and she desperately wants to avoid the embarrassment and shame. She equally wants to avoid the treatment she is sure to receive as a witness facing the accused. "I know how this works, I see it every day. They put them [the victims] on the witness stand and crucify them, and then laugh about it."

The woman in the 1961 film is a "drifter" who knows the justice system will not be able to protect her when Max Cady is released and hunts her down for testifying against him. Responding to the authorities' urgings that she file charges against Cady, the victim explains, "You can't help me. Six months and after that (pause) When he walked out of this room, he said to consider this only a sample. And from my limited knowledge of human nature, Max Cady isn't a man who makes idle threats."

Sam, in both versions, explains why Cady stalks his daughter, not just his wife in terms of the balance the court must maintain between the rights of the accused and the victims of sexual violence. Cady does not simply want to vilify Sam's property, he has calculated a way to escape prosecuting. The child will be put on the witness stand—Cady will face his accuser. On the witness stand, the child will be broken down—portrayed either as a precocious, promiscuous teen or as a fantasizing child. Sam believes that Cady knows he would never put his daughter through this painful ordeal.

In 1961, the mother, arriving early to pick up her daughter at school, leaves her car parked while she walks down the street to the grocery. What in reality may have been only a few minutes, turns into a frightening drawn-out chase scene. Abandoned and completely unprotected, the daughter believes she sees "the big man with the cigar" coming toward her to hurt her. She leaves the car, runs to hide in the school, and the chilling chase scene that follows turns out to be in her imagination—the man chasing her down the hallway is really only the janitor walking through the building. The camera doesn't show his face until the end; instead it focuses on his groin as he slowly walks toward her. Not able to see him from her hiding place, she runs in terror from the school building, right into Cady's arms as he waits, stalking her outside. Breaking away she then runs into the path of an oncoming car.

This scene is a metaphor of sexual terror and a depiction of sexual terror's oppression. Although she is not actually chased by Cady, it is not merely her imagination either. He is there, but he is not the specific one who walks behind her. He merely waits for her. It would be wrong to say she terrorizes herself, but the subtle terror Cady's presence conveys, leads to her irrational, unintentional burst into the car's path. He "does nothing" in this scene but look at her. He has already laid the foundation of terror that causes her "self destruction."

In the end, Max Cady is defeated, no thanks to law and order or the justice system. Sam, the patriarch, must take matters into his own hands. In 1961 he tries to do this first by simply going after Cady with a hand gun. His wife stops him, giving a moralizing sermon on patriarchal justice, the rights of the accused, and the duty of a defense attorney—Sam's oath—and the practical argument that Sam will become a murderer.

In both movies adults devise a complicated scheme to lure Cady up the Cape Fear River with daughter and wife as bait, leaving Sam to do battle with Cady's evilness. In both films the daughter and wife also do battle with Cady, their unsuccessful efforts reinforcing the portrayal of women as powerless. In 1961, Sam remains loyal to patriarchal law and, when given the opportunity to kill Cady, chooses to let him live. By 1991 fidelity to law mattered less than single-handedly subduing evil.

The original film ends with the family somberly driving down the river in their speedboat, with the father having created a safer world by his faithfulness to the rule of law. The Scorsese film ends with the family huddled in mud on the beach with the daughter's voice-over testifying to the horror's long-term effect on the family and on her psyche.

The portrayal of evil is markedly different in these two films, reflecting a significant change in attitudes about evil and violence between 1961 and 1991. A comparison of both films with "Twin Peaks" underscores these changes in social attitudes. In "Twin Peaks" evil, not human beings, is the culpable perpetrator of sexual violence. In the 1991 *Cape Fear*, evil is often likeable, or, at least, only confusing. Good is not innocent, and neither construct stands dichotomously against the other. In 1961, a sexual encounter of any sort between an adult and a teen was assumed to be wrong. In 1991, we can imagine the teenage daughter being seduced, perhaps even inviting Cady's sexual advances. In 1991, Cady threatens the father with sexual terror directed at the women in the family; he makes sexual advances toward the teenager. In 1961, Cady threatens violence of a sexual nature. Thirty years later, sexual violence fits between evil and good in a new continuum of hazy morality. One thing remains constant in all of these films: patriarchy continues to reign as master and victor.

FILM: REPRESENTATION AND VEHICLE OF THE SEXUAL/POLITICAL VIOLENCE NEXUS

Sexual terror is political terror, serving as the medium through which even liberal authority is enforced. These media portrayals of political violence prime the depths of personal threat, not only drawing on, but also transforming, the personal into the political. Inundated with fused images, we no longer can definitively separate our personal experience from the equally persuasive "reality" created by the authoritative voice of the media. Framing the message of political violence in sexual terms, news and entertainment media create a cultural synthesis of sex and violence. Combined with the use of symbolic imagery and language, this entire amalgamation forms the constructs for developing personal narratives uniting sexual terror and political violence. Personal narratives and public narratives interact and reinforce the potency of each field's message. Although our personal experience may not include being victimized by sexual violence, no private reality escapes the cultural narrative of these threats.

In a culture of terrorism, sexual terror is pivotal to political violence. Stored in our memories, our internalized memories, attitudes, and images of sexual violence can be consciously and unconsciously activated by direct and indirect public discourse, metaphor, or action. When information is presented or framed in a specific way, as in the public narrative of war, these memories and images are stimulated, or primed, and influence our political judgments. When our private "war stories" also include personal experiences and stored memories of sexual terror, they fuse with the public narratives and jointly influence our interpretations of sexual and political violence. Our private war stories of sexual terror, therefore, are susceptible to being activated unobtrusively by public war stories.

The enemy of sexual terror is nameless and escapeless. In "Twin Peaks" culpability is assigned to the devil. In *Cape Fear* (1991), God's self-proclaimed avenger causes the evil that men do. Yet in politics we control what cannot be controlled in our private terrors. In the opening narrative, "Khrushchev" gave visage, dimension, and motive to evil. A quarter century later, the vilified "evil empire," Russia, similarly provided meaning for our fears. Evil, now personified, could be ruled through technology, might, and right.

Such formulas are nowadays commonplace as news media take a cue from broadcast fiction creating "info-tainment" by mounting "productions" of actual events such as CNN's Gulf War reporting and NBC's "America Held Hostage," as well as the ABC nightly news show "Nightline." Such framing is possible because our indelible private movies, self-produced by personal experiences of terror, are subject to priming by media. Media draw on these events and the culture of threat to frame how we make sense of public narratives, forever coloring the lens for viewing our world. TV news can prime or activate personal narratives of terror by broadcasting, in "living color," public narratives of terror.

The public arena of political violence is a composite and creator of these private narratives, drawing from and superimposing frameworks that explain the personal. Any attempt to create a narrative to "make sense" of personal trauma is influenced by the public arena's construction that superimposes meaning on our personal terrors, which in reality, lack "sense."

Fusing sexual violence and political violence in public narratives through metaphor, action, and the replay of war stories blurs the distinction between legitimate force and violence, reducing our capacity to think critically, limit the exercise of authority, and govern ourselves. If political violence is understood as a necessary evil in our world, it is hard to imagine that similar acceptance is not extended to sexual violence. The insidious fusion of sex and violence limits the likelihood that sexual violence will be diminished in society. Rather than exploring the public dimension of sexual violence, this link masks the true nature of sex and violence, distorting our judgment about what is private and what is public and the use of force in either sphere. The fusion of sexual and political violence creates a culture of terror, making the threat of sexual violence the background of daily life.

Gender dominance perpetuates the idea that the only kind of power is paternalistic power over others. Such a conception hardly lends itself to revolutionizing ideas about designs for real political authority. Rather than electing an alternative candidate for political authority, the incumbent, patriarchy, remains in power. So long as this is the case, sexual violence remains integral to political rule. Vulnerable to threats of violence in the personal and political spheres, women are more likely to be annihilated by the holocaust of rape than by nuclear war.

NOTES

1. Mani Kamerkar personal correspondence, December 31, 1992, Bombay India; Peter Goodspeed, "India's Human Rights Record under Fire: Suspects Raped, Tortured Routinely While in Police Custody, Group Says," *Toronto Star*, January 31, 1993, F 2.; "Mass Rape in War; Prosecute The Guilty," *The Ottawa Citizen*, January 17, 1993, B1.

2. Stanley Rosenberg, "The Threshold of Thrill: Life Stories in the Skies over Southeast Asia," in Miriam Cooke and Angela Woollacott, eds., *Gendering War Talk* (Princeton, NJ: Princeton University Press, 1993).

3. Susan Jeffords, *The Remasculinization of America: Gender and the Vietnam War* (Bloomington: Indiana University Press, 1990).

4. Klaus Theweleit, "The Bomb's Womb and the Genders of War (War Goes on Preventing Women from Becoming Mothers of Invention)," in Miriam Cooke and Angela Woollacott, eds., *Gendering War Talk*, 1993, 284.

5. Laura Mulvey, "Visual Pleasure and Narrative Cinema," in Patricia Erens, ed., *Issues in Feminist Film Criticisma* (Bloomington: Indiana University Press, 1990), 30. This theory of the gaze stems from the idea of scopophilia in Lacanian psychoanalytic theory.

6. Ibid.

7. Just war criteria illustrate this claim. The just war criteria state that war must be declared by a legitimate authority, must be undertaken to promote good

or prevent evil, and must be a proportional defensive response to the harm committed by the opposition. In war, moral thinking about justice also informs the definition of noncombatants through rules of engagement.

8. *Un Chien Andalou* can be compared with the television show "Twin Peaks," which also exploits the impact of sexual violence on the viewer. "Twin Peaks's" depiction of sexual violence, however, erodes the surrealists' political purpose to the point of complicity with ongoing cultural and political violence. A comparison of "Twin Peaks's" regressive, entertainment-motivated use of sexual violence to *Un Chien Andalou* is all the more appropriate because of "Twin Peaks's" intertextual references to *Un Chien Andalou.*

9. Susan Rubin Suleiman, *Subversive Intent: Gender, Politics, and the Avant-Garde* (Cambridge, MA: Harvard University Press, 1990), xv.

10. Ibid., 34–36.

11. Linda Williams, *Figures of Desire: A Theory and Analysis of Surrealist Film* (Urbana: University of Illinois Press, 1981). This gives one of the most complete discussions of this work as a methodological model of this sort of analysis. See also Sulieman.

12. Williams, 69–73.

13. Ibid., 72.

14. Ibid., 73.

15. The author thanks Sue A. Lafky for conversations and for sharing unpublished work from her extensive research on the cultural meaning of "Twin Peaks" in the context of the Reagan years.

16. Theodore Adorno and Max Horkheimer, "The Culture Industry: Enlightenment and Mass Deception," in John Cummings, ed., *Dialectic of Enlightenment* (New York: Continuum,, 1982), 120–67.

17. Joshua Hammer, "From Peaks to Valleys: Does Anyone Still Care Who Killed Laura Palmer?" *Newsweek*, November 19, 1990, 76.

18. The show attracted so much of a following that ABC has now made it available on home video, allowing students who did not watch the first run on television to view the series and participate in classroom discussions about its content.

19. Quoted in Martha Southgate, " 'Twin Peaks': TV's Walk on the Weird Side," *New York Daily News*, May 20, 1990.

20. Howard Hampton, "Blue Velveeta: David Lynch's Dead-End Street of Dreams," *Minneapolis City Pages*, November 19, 1992, 10.

21. *The Nation,* " 'Twin Peaks,' U.S.A.," June 11, 1990, 808.

22. Sue A. Lafky, "Gender and Power in the Televisual World of Post-Reagan America: A Feminist Critique of 'Twin Peaks,'" unpublished manuscript, 1993.

23. Mark A. Altman, *Twin Peaks: Behind the Scenes* (Las Vegas: Pioneer Books, Inc., 1990), 23.

24. Bill Zehme, "Babes in the Woods," *Rolling Stone*, October 4, 1990, 68.

25. Craig Owens, "The Discourse of Others: Feminists and Postmodernism," in Hal Foster, ed., *The Anti-Aesthetic: Essays on Postmodern Culture* (Seattle: Bay Press, 1983), 70.

26. As quoted in Altman, 1990, 130.

27. Ibid.

28. Ibid.

4

Shattered but Not Broken: Images of Structural Violence and War by Black Women Filmmakers

Gloria J. Gibson

Structural violence distinguishes the African American experience.
—*Juliet E. K. Walker*

One of the most remarked upon but least analyzed themes in Black women's history deals with Black women's sexual vulnerability and powerlessness as victims of rape and domestic violence.
—*Darlene Clark Hine*

Black people worldwide continue to struggle against past vestiges and contemporary manifestations of structural violence and war. In the Americas, the Caribbean, and Europe, Africans were relegated to chattel and sold into slavery. In Africa, the tyranny of institutionalized colonialization imposed a system of personal and societal displacement that continues to haunt many African nations and people of African descent even today. In regard to black women, the devastation of war and structural violence remains crucial for societal and academic investigation.

Cinema can function as a powerful medium through which to study the various effects and manifestations of oppression. Whether documentary or narrative, film has the potential to introduce audiences to the everyday life and reality of the world's peoples and to communicate specifically how those people cope with the day-to-day realities of structural violence and war. This chapter seeks to answer critical questions such as: how do women filmmakers explicate the nature of violence and war; whose voice becomes the primary vehicle for communicating women's struggle against hegemony, sexism, marginality, and other disruptive social forces; and what cinematic techniques do artists utilize for communicating their messages? As this chapter addresses these questions, it establishes the importance of black women filmmakers' cinematic cultural critiques. Their work captures the effects and resultant implications of structural violence and war. Most important, however, is the fact that even though filmmakers expose fragments of "shattered" lives, they also unearth survival strategies women have employed to circumvent, in some cases, utter destruction.

Specifically, this chapter will discuss the following films: *Sidet: Forced Exile* (Salem Mekuria, 1991, Ethiopia), *Suzanne, Suzanne* (James V. Hatch and Camille Billops, 1982, United States), *And Still I Rise* (Ngozi Onwurah, 1991, Britain), and *Kumekucha: From Sun Up* (Flora M'Mbugu-Schelling, 1987, Tanzania). Each filmmaker wrote, produced, and directed her film. These films were selected because they authoritatively challenge existing dominant conventions of structural violence against women. Although the genres vary, each film: (1) acknowledges the complexity of black women's lives; and (2) invokes and realizes a vision of black womanhood situated within a social, cultural, and political framework. The conceptual areas to be explored are: structural violence and slavery, domestic violence, and manifestations of exile and war. The films, while entertaining, are not "art for art's sake." As these cinematic expressions acknowledge violence against women, they concurrently seek the betterment of women's societal conditions.

SLAVERY AS STRUCTURAL VIOLENCE

The condition of slavery remains one of the most horrifying examples of institutionalized structural violence in American history. Juliet E.K. Walker notes, "Since 1619, countless injuries and an incalculable number of deaths from slavery and racism have had devastating consequences for blacks in America."[1] Legitimized by religious doctrine, scientific precepts, patriarchal attitudes, and paternalistic behaviors, slavery unleashed a legacy of incalculable suffering, the reverberations of which are still being realized today. As a form of structural violence, slavery sanctioned, and to some extent promoted, the mistreatment of blacks. Slaves were property—subject to untold brutality and often death. The violence manifest itself in the forms of mental, physical, and sexual abuse.

African women were also victims, subjected to the control of white men, whose power extended to black women's sexuality as they functioned as the abject instrument of their master's desires. While physical abuse in the form of rape was practically intolerable, psychological damage in the form of demeaning propaganda reflected the innate viciousness of the oppressor. Psychological abuse revolved around the transmission of an ideology of black women as biologically inferior and sexually promiscuous. While invisible shackles of slavery have long since disappeared, visible shackles of slavery continue to penetrate the consciousness of many African-American women.

Hazel Carby provides historical background, explaining:

The effect of black female sexuality on the white male was represented in an entirely different form from that of the figurative power of white female sexuality. Confronted by the black woman, the white man behaved in a manner that was considered to be entirely untempered by any virtuous qualities; the white male, in fact, was represented as being merely prey to the rampant sexuality of his female slaves.[2]

Consequently, as bell hooks notes, "devaluation of black womanhood occurred as a result of the sexual exploitation of black women during slavery that has not altered in the course of hundreds of years."[3] To justify their violation of black women, white men imposed a cultural identity upon African women slaves that dehumanized them. Denying the humanity of black women sanctioned all manner of physical, mental, and sexual cruelty on the part of white men. Thus, the stereotype of black woman as sexual savage emerged and prospered. Even after slavery, white attitudes and behaviors toward black women changed little. Perceiving them as sluts, mammies, or tragic mulattoes legitimized the harsh treatment of black women levied by white men and women. Not only was the black woman devalued, but because of societal perception, her subsequent film image held negligible cinematic value.[4]

Black independent filmmakers worldwide tend to "reimage" the black cinematic icon. In this way there is a dramatic shift away from predetermined roles and one-dimensional stereotypes. Independent filmmaking also presents a new way of seeing and filming womanhood. In viewing and analysing the films, the experience becomes a more encompassing visualization. Film can not only impart basic information, it potentially can influence attitudes and behaviors. As such, cinema becomes a political tool for enlightenment, activism, and empowerment.

STRUCTURAL VIOLENCE AND SLAVERY: *AND STILL I RISE*

The films of black British filmmakers reimage (mis)representation by presenting cinematic representations that counter mainstream images. Black British scholar Kobena Mercer acknowledges:

A cursory survey of the work of black filmmakers in Britain will reveal the preponderance of a "realist" aesthetic in films made within both documentary and narrative genres. This insistent emphasis on the real must be understood as the prevailing mode in which independent black film has performed a critical function in providing a counter-discourse against those versions of reality produced by dominant voices and discourses in British film and media.[5]

One counter-discourse theme is violence against women. While this theme has appeared in literature, its emergence in cinema is recent. Hine notes in regard to black women's literature, "themes of rape and sexual vulnerability have received considerable attention in the recent literary outpourings of Black women novelists."[6] She continues, "Of the last six novels I have read and reread, five contained a rape scene or a graphic description of domestic violence. Moreover, this is not a recent phenomenon in Black women's writings."[7] In recent years more and more films follow the lead of literature by incorporating images of violence against women.

First and foremost, Ngozi Onwurah's *And Still I Rise* cautions black women to understand how myths concerning sexuality and sensuality have been utilized to infer an identity of promiscuity, licentiousness, and inferiority. Race and gender sentenced black women not only to subjugation, but, sadly, in many cases the (mis)representation and appropriation of her own body contributed to an injurious self-concept. The film is framed within the context of historic and contemporary British society, exploring the psychological damage of racism, sexism, and classism. Through staged dramatizations and candid interviews, the film surveys how stereotypes have been historically internalized and subsequently exorcised.

And Still I Rise is informed by and incorporates the messages of the celebrated poem of the same title by the acclaimed African-American writer Maya Angelou. Like Angelou's poem, Onwurah's film is saturated with and situated in history—black women's history. The structure of the film combines documentary and dramatized segments. The documentary sections allow black women of diverse backgrounds to reflect on the relationship between black women's sexuality and identity formation. The dramatic reconstructions, framed as memories of slave women on the selling blocks and violent rape, implicate racist societal structures for the devastating indictments and pronouncements against black womanhood.

Onwurah's initial cinematic image is that of a black woman in African garb walking in a meadow. That image of a proud, beautiful black woman, who could be from the past or contemporary, is juxtaposed to a soundtrack that spews contemptuous myths and negative stereotypes about black women. The voice-over begins with one word descriptors: sultry, savage, dirty, hard, exotic, erotic. These words and their accompanying conceptual myths potentially erode self-esteem and construct a world suffused with self-doubt.

Later in the film, Onwurah, using film clips of Lisa Bonet in *Angel Heart* and Grace Jones in *Vamp*, demonstrates how the image of the sexual savage has been incorporated into contemporary cinema. In both films the women are exotic, erotic, and demonic. Bonet is murdered when a gun is discharged into her vagina. This act becomes symbolic of the destructiveness of white oppression and its need to eradicate or control black women's sexuality and black women in general. These films and others perpetuate a destructive cycle of misrepresentation. Negative, one-dimensional societal attitudes structure demeaning cinematic imagery, and powerless, cinematic icons feed and reinforce fallacious societal perception. More than "just misconceptions," one-dimensional myths of black womanhood contain an inherent danger, namely:

Representations of powerlessness have an effect on those in control: they give them the authority to continue to suppress collective resistance through force. Most importantly, images of powerlessness have an effect on those who would resist: rather than giving them incentive to further action, they may prompt an acceptance of the status quo.[8]

And Still I Rise dramatizes a rape sequence during slavery. When a black woman exercises courage by refusing a gift and spitting in her master's face, he brutally rapes her, interpreting her screams of pain as sounds of enjoyment. After this savagery, he returns to his wife, sitting in tranquility. The wife no doubt has heard the assault. The voice-over explains that white slave owners viewed their female slaves as livestock, which had to be "broken-in." As research indicates, rape is not an act of sexual pleasure, but an act of violence, a perverted psychological need for power. The scene, framed as a memory flashback, demystifies rape by clearly dramatizing the slave woman not as a willing collaborator but as a powerless victim.

The film's structure also incorporates interviews from black women, who, through self-reflection, discuss the psychological dimensions of identity formation. Novelist Buchi Emecheta explains that black women's identity and sexuality are derived from an African heritage. She states the following in the film:

Your umbilical cord from Africa has not been cut and it can never be cut because your blackness is like a badge—you wear it wherever you are. You must not suppress your Africanness. You don't have to be in Africa to live in Africa, to identify with Africa. Wherever you are you carry your Africa with you.

Emecheta and Onwurah recognize and remember that Africa is the motherland, and through identification with their heritage a more profound sense of self emerges. Remembering and reflecting on the source—the essence of one's being—leads to empowerment. To exorcise the pain and self-doubt, black women must rise above oppressive, racist strategies.

Onwurah concludes the film with black women reciting Angelou's poem. The first stanza reads:

> You may write me down in history
> With your bitter, twisted lies,
> You may trod me in the very dirt
> But still, like dust, I'll rise.

The line "I rise," is repeated three times at the end of the poem as the film underscores the importance of this line. Black women and a little black girl, who symbolically steps out of a cage, proclaim, "I rise." Onwurah's *And Still I Rise* is reminiscent of a lyrical text with its fragmented images and lines that poeticize and politicize the images of black womanhood.

Onwurah's film deconstructs the hegemonic voice regarding black women's history, identity, and sexuality. Mainstream images of black women generally render them cinematically as one-dimensional and de-historicized. Onwurah's dramatized representations of historic mistreatment and candid statements by interviewees reaffirm womanhood by situating black women's identities as a manifestation of diasporic history. In addition, *And Still I Rise* foregrounds the uncomfortable memories of rape and misrepresentation. Through reflection, however, the women communicate to audiences the realization that patriarchal behaviors and images embody power if women allow them to do so.

DOMESTIC VIOLENCE: *SUZANNE, SUZANNE* AND *FROM SUN UP*

Domestic violence, in its diverse manifestations, remains one of the most complex forms of oppression. In fact, statistics reveal that in many instances violence against women and children is not even reported, rendering it an almost "invisible" form of tyranny. In some cultures, acts of domestic violence are not defined as such; rather they are a "privilege" of the husband. Moreover, women and children suffer silently because of fear. This section will explore films that highlight forms of domestic violence: Kumekucha: *From Sun Up* by Tanzania filmmaker Flora M'Mbugu-Schelling and *Suzanne, Suzanne* by James V. Hatch and Camille Billops. Two different forms of abuse are explored: the first is gross neglect of the family, which results in psychological and economic hardship; the second is physical abuse, which also generates psychological problems.

Both forms of abuse, physical/sexual or neglect/abandonment are encased within power struggles. Both result in women's subordinate status and possibly their subsequent restricted access to economic power. As women are subjected to sometimes unbearable forms of structural violence in the forms of racism, sexism, and homophobia, they may also be subjected to violence in their home. Statistics reveal that black women are much more likely to experience abusive violence than white women. For example, the rate of abusive violence toward black women in 1985 was slightly more than twice the rate of severe violence toward white women. Perhaps more important than numbers is the realization that scholars identify various types of physical abuse. Sociologist Michael P. Johnson distinguishes between two forms of physical violence stating:

There are two distinct forms of couple violence taking place in American households. Evidence from large-sample survey research and from data gathered from women's shelters and other public agencies suggests that a large number of families suffer from occasional outbursts of violence from either husbands or wives or both, while a significant number of other families are terrorized by systematic male violence enacted in the service of patriarchal control.[9]

What differentiates Johnson's research is his distinction between sporadic violence and patriarchal terrorism. Patriarchal implies it is endemic to societal structure, perhaps to male socialization; terrorism implies the abuse is violent, laced with fear. Control becomes the most salient operative factor in the process.

No less tragic is violence against children. Statistics reveal the child abuse rate was significantly higher in households where wife battering occurred than in non-wife-battering households.[10] Further, "the rates of severe violence toward black children were higher in 1985 than in 1975."[11] From 1990–1994 according to the *Statistical Abstract of the United States*, substantiated violent crimes against women and the cases of child abuse and neglect continued to increase. These statistics indicate that various forms of domestic violence continue to be a serious problem in the United States.

Using various cinematic techniques such as film-within-film, montage, and candid interviews, Billops constructs a free-form documentary to expose the issue of physical abuse and to serve as a cathartic vehicle for healing. Black-and white-film contributes to the cultural realism and intimate texture of *Suzanne, Suzanne*. Integrating personal narratives communicates and reinforces Suzanne's perception of the abuse. Most importantly, as the physical abuse is unearthed, so, too, is the resultant psychological damage to the mother and the daughter. Ironically, the familial relationships under the microscope are her own relatives.

Billops presents, interprets, and helps the audience understand physical violence. By illuminating the manifestations of abuse, she builds a bridge to the audience. The film captures the story through voice inflection, body language, and kinesic behavior. Although the film becomes increasingly more distressing, Billops initially places the audience at ease because she begins with the abuser's funeral, assuring the viewers that the father can no longer physically harm the family. Suzanne's paradox becomes one of reconciling the sorrow of his death and the joy in knowing the abuse is over.

Suzanne's psychological trauma is apparent by the questions she poses at the beginning of the film as Browne, her father, lies repose. She asks, "Did you love me? Why did you treat me the way you did? Why did you take out your hostility on me? Why did I always get whippings and nobody else? Couldn't you just hug me and tell me you cared for me?" Finally she admits, "When he died and he took that last breath, I gave a sigh of relief." While it may be unclear whether Suzanne's father loved her, it is clear that she rarely felt the love and support she yearned. Suzanne's voice-over undergirds images of old family photographs that are cracked, tattered, and torn, symbolic of the family's deteriorated relationship.

The physical abuse caused Suzanne more than physical pain. She later states, "I felt so bad about myself—I thought I was ugly, stupid." Her feelings of inadequacy led to drug dependency and other self-destructive behaviors. In several scenes where she demeans herself, as well as many others throughout the film, Suzanne permeates the center of the frame. Situating her in this way functions as an important film technique. Diawara explains, "Space is related to power and powerlessness, in so far as those who occupy the center of the screen are usually more powerful than those situated in the background or completely absent from the screen."[12] At this point in the film, Suzanne's image, center screen, embodies and symbolizes power to the audience. As such, her icon is empowering to other women who are struggling with violence in the home.

As the film continues, it becomes apparent that the father was abusive to both the mother and daughter. Suzanne asks her mother, "Did daddy beat you from the beginning? Was it the same as being on death row?" These questions and the subsequent mother/daughter confrontation frame the most dramatic and painful portion of the film. In her article, Valerie Smith explains: "At this point, Billie's head shifts and her facial expression changes, apparently signaling a recognition of shared circumstances. Not only were both victims of physical violence, but also endured the psychological terror of imagining and awaiting each instance of Browne's abuse.[13]

For a child and mother to refer to physical abuse as "death row" indicates the depth of their terror. The women equate the actual abuse to death, but the waiting is additionally laced with agony. Their fallacy in using death row as a metaphor for their beatings is that criminals are placed on death row because they have committed a serious crime—they have been judged and sentenced by a jury of their peers. Within the family structure, Browne functions as judge and jury, sentencing his wife and child to unprovoked and unwarranted "punishment." Waiting becomes a form of intimidation and emotional abuse—physical violence becomes the ultimate vehicle of power and control.

The overt manifestations of abuse in *Suzanne, Suzanne* can be situated on a continuum with other forms of abuse, such as family neglect. Neglect takes the form of emotional, financial, and total separation from the family. Each of these forms causes stress to the wife and children. In many instances it is the wife who is left to provide the child with emotional as well as financial support.

In many parts of Africa, structured servitude is a vital part of the society. Nancy J. Haflin and Edna G. Bay note, in *Women in Africa: Studies in Social and Economic Change*, that, "structural constraints to limit women's potential may have developed as societies moved toward greater male dominance."[14] They further assert that, in many countries, certain cultural practices function to ensure and legitimize the subordination and oppression of women. Whether social or traditional law, the effect remains the same—women's lives become fractured in gender systems that are structured to benefit men.

In regard to film, Manthia Diawara notes that an important recurring theme in Third World Cinema is that of the struggle for the emancipation of women. Diawara states, "The social realist cinema also positions the spectator by addressing the issues of women's liberation in contemporary African society. The films show that while African men have accepted progress in certain areas of modernism, they are regressive when it comes to giving up male privileges."[15]

M'Mbugu-Schelling's *From Sun Up* (1987) is a documentary which paints a compelling portrait of African women farmers in Tanzania. The themes of sexual oppression, economic importance, and female bonding emerge as significant political and humanistic motifs. The film vividly communicates the fact that women's basic survival is a daily struggle. M'Mbugu -Schelling's cinematic depiction concurs with findings of an in-depth study indicating that "roughly 87% of all Tanzanian women live in the countryside. The bulk of women's economic activity is related to peasant agricultural production and rural household reproduction."16 The low economic status of many women is further exacerbated because they have absent husbands or do not own the land on which they toil in the fields from sunup to sunset in order to provide for themselves and their children. They realize, however, that they must not and cannot succumb physically or psychologically to everyday pressures. M'Mgubu-Schelling captures the powerlessness in their lives, but she also addresses how the women overcome seemingly insurmountable odds to care for themselves and their children.

M'Mbugu -Schelling examines two critical issues during her interviews with women: (1) the effects of sexism and class that impede economic growth; and (2) the development of survival mechanisms, such as women's farm collectives, which help to counteract the gnawing pangs of poverty. The film is not an indictment against men. Conversely, it communicates the need for women and men to be aware of and sensitive to the degradation of economic impotence and sexual humiliation. Exploring the effects of sexism and class structure reveals a more meaningful culture-specific message that can potentially result in enlightenment and reform.

Capturing the women's experiences of film enables the viewer to witness their discussion of life's vicissitudes. One woman states: "Nowadays life has become difficult. I have four children. My life depends on small businesses. I brew beer to earn money for food and clothes." Ironically, the women, in many cases, sell beer to each other's husbands. The film details how some men will buy beer from women and, at the same time, fail to support their own families. The narrator concludes, "Beer carries a steep social price."

Despite the minuscule salaries of Tanzanian women, "wage labour objectively offers an independent subsistence separate from male control. A small but significant number of women wage-earners have subjectively rejected marriage and binding relationships with men, and in so doing are creating new family patterns."17 *From Sun Up* documents how women, realizing their individual powerlessness, band together to assist and support one another. They organize into collectives, helping each other produce and sell their beer. This spirit of cooperation allows each woman to make money to feed her children. "We have organized to help ourselves and our children. Still we do not move forward; we stand still." Another woman confides, "We help each other a lot, we help each other to carry on this difficult life and lift each other up when one falls." As the women discuss their individual problems that are shared by others, they become empowered through organizing and bonding. The film documents how they firmly stand in opposition to the oppressive status quo.

From Sun Up captures the remarkable courage and determination of Tanzanian women as they strive to survive day by day. The film ends, not in despair, but with hope, as the women realize that they will all survive if they support one another. Developing and strengthening women's solidarity will eventually culminate in the emergence of cohesive strategies for survival. M'Mbugu-Schelling believes that if Tanzanian women and men make a concerted effort to understand their past and present conditions, their future can improve.

WAR AND BANISHMENT, *SIDET: FORCED EXILE*

Salem Mekuria, an Ethiopian filmmaker now living in the United States, traveled back to her homeland to produce *Sidet: Forced Exile*. Tracing the lives of three Ethiopian women refugees living in the Sudan, the documentary communicates how, "particularly in a region characterized by poverty and exploitation, some groups have been even more oppressed than others—landless peasants, the minority nationalities, Muslims and *all* women" [my emphasis].[18] Through Mekuria's lens, the audience is introduced to the women's struggles and their methods of self-empowerment.

The documentary format, once again, allows the informants to speak for themselves—to tell their own stories that interpret and communicate the impact of historic issues, political processes, and remembered events. However, even within their status as "other"—as exile—diversity exists. Social critic Florence Ladd notes in her film review of *Sidet*:

The women differ with respect to personalities, education, family responsibilities, coping strategies, and capacity to establish themselves and their families in a foreign country. Their differences suggest that women refugees are not a monolithic group; each, with her unique strengths and weaknesses, is at the mercy of national and international forces that tear lives asunder.[19]

Although the women embody difference, all three are refugees.

The documentary genre also permits the audience to align itself with each woman's dilemma in a realistic fashion. Mekuria states of the filmic format, "The piece is basically structured in portraits of individual women, and through them I intend to explore social and political issues. Their voices are guiding me through it."[20] Because the undergirding structure establishes the women's voices within a sociohistorical context, the film embraces a realist style. As Bill Nichols notes:

the realist style in documentary grounds the text in the historical world. It is a mark of authenticity, testifying to the camera, and hence the filmmaker, having "been there" and thus providing the warrant for our own "being there," viewing the historical world through the transparent amber of indexical images and realist style.[21]

Consequently, through the documentary genre and a female-centered realist style, the women's testimonies and remembrances are not subjugated to those of anyone else.

Mekuria allows the women to reflect on their circumstances and identities before and after the war. For example, an elderly woman performing at the beginning of the film sings about her life: "I'm thirsty, my sister, I'm hungry, my mother. Who can I tell this to? I'm in exile. Oh me, oh my, in silence all season, I have nothing at all except old age and my poverty." As she sings, the camera pans to juxtapose the text of the song with the barren social space of the women. The film becomes more than "talking heads" as shots are framed to include a backdrop of devastation. In other scenes Mekuria utilizes long shots that also establish women in hostile environments.

Terhas, one of the women interviewed, remembers her life before exile when she considered herself prosperous. That identity was shattered when she was injured fleeing from Ethiopia and was later abandoned by her husband, leaving her to provide for five children. As she recounts her story, her memories are laced with pain. Those memories serve as the bridge to monitor her transformation. Rather than succumbing to the suffering, she uses these memories in a self-reflexive manner to change the future through her children. Terhas encourages them to succeed in school and she begins a catering service to generate income.

In her article "Common Themes, Different Contexts," Cheryl Johnson-Odim observes

In 'underdeveloped' societies it is not just a question of internal redistribution of resources, but of their generation and control; not just equal opportunity between men and women but the creation of opportunity itself; not just the position of women in society, but the position of the societies in which Third World women find themselves.[22]

Mekuria's documentary examines not only the impact of structural poverty on women in exile, but also the specific repercussions of these detrimental conditions that are further exacerbated by prolonged war.

Through intimate discussions with three women, *Sidet: Forced Exile* explores how (1) the experience of war has affected identity formation; (2) introspection leads to a heightened awareness and identity (re)formation; (3) identity empowerment results when marginality and passivity are replaced with resilience and persistence. Mekuria uses film to capture multidimensional aspects of exile as women strive for individual and collective freedom. Cultural memory becomes a tool to not only question identity but to mediate new relationships with others and, most importantly, with "woman-self."

CONCLUSION

The films of black women can play an instrumental role in examining the various manifestations of structure violence and war. The films become an intimate account, through women's eyes, of their struggles and triumphs. The personal is the political. The politicalization of black womanhood is achieved because films are informed by aspects of race, gender, and class. Because the films are female-centered, this focus permits filmmakers to place characters in situations through which they develop survival imperatives and grow to a stronger sense of self.

The women tell their own stories. The filmmakers listen and project women's voices. Audience members are presented with self-portraits of characters and individuals that capture the innermost thoughts and worldview of black womanhood. Most importantly, in each film, the narrative is accurately interwoven with sociocultural history.

Finally, each film demonstrates the resilience of black women as they rise above an oppressive status quo through self-examination and self-affirmation. In black women's film tradition, personal transformation becomes a significant element. Black women filmmakers capture the voices of women struggling to develop survival imperatives to overcome victimization—or, at the very least, fight against it. These films do not have fairy tale "everybody lives happily ever after" conclusions as deeply seeded problems related to racism, sexism, and classism do not have quick easy solutions.

In conclusion, black women, worldwide, struggle against various manifestations of structural violence. Violence has been a dominant thread in their history since slavery. Black women's films expose these significant historical, cultural, and social issues. Moreover, audiences are encouraged to understand how the film characters' interpersonal interactions, subsequent maturation, and empowerment on the screen can function to strengthen their own personal knowledge and consciousness. Scholarly research not only contributes to a better understanding of their films, but, in part, helps to communicate to others the need to improve the status of black women worldwide.

NOTES

1. Juliet E.K. Walker, "War, Peace, and Structural Violence: Peace Activism and the African-American Historic Experience," Occasional Paper no. 14, (Indiana Center on Global Change and World Peace, Indiana University, Bloomington, July 1992), 1.

2. Hazel Carby, *Reconstructing Womanhood: The Emergence of the Afro-American Woman Novelist* (New York: Oxford University Press, 1987), 27.

3. bell hooks, *Ain't I a Woman: Black Women and Feminism* (Boston: South End Press, 1981), 53.

4. See the following for discussion of stereotypes of African-American women: Robyn Wiegman, "Black Bodies/American Commodities: Gender, Race, and the Bourgeois Ideal in Contemporary Film," in Lester Friedman, ed., *Unspeakable Images: Ethnicity and the American Cinema* (Urbana: University of Illinois Press, 1991); Elizabeth Hadley Friedberg, "Prostitutes, Concubines, Whores, and Bitches: Black and Hispanic Women in Contemporary Film," in Audrey McCluskey, ed., *Women of Color: Perspectives on Feminism and Identity* (Bloomington: Women's Studies Program, Indiana University, 1985); Pearl Bowser, "Sexual Imagery and the Black Woman in Cinema," in Gladstone L. Yearwood, ed., *Black Cinema Aesthetics: Issues in Independent Black Filmmaking* (Athens, OH: Center for Afro-American Studies, Ohio University, 1982); Donald Bogle, *Toms, Coons, Mulattoes, Mammies, and Bucks* (New York: Continuum, 1990).

5. Kobena Mercer, "Diaspora Culture and the Dialogic Imagination: The Aesthetic of Black Independent Film in Britain," in Mbye B. Cham and Claire Andrade-Watkins, eds., *Blackframes: Critical Perspectives on Black Independent Cinema* (Cambridge, MA: MIT Press, 1988), 52.

6. Darlene Clark Hine, "Rape and the Inner Lives of Black Women in the Middle West: Preliminary Thoughts on the Culture of Dissemblance," in Ellen Carol DuBois and Vicki L. Ruiz, eds., *Unequal Sisters: A Multicultural Reader in U.S. Women's History* (New York: Routledge, 1990), 293.

7. Ibid., 292.

8. Jacqueline Bobo, "Black Women in Fiction and Nonfiction: Images of Power and Powerlessness," in *Wide Angle* 13, nos. 3–4 (July-October 1991), 73.

9. Michael P. Johnson, "Patriarchal Terrorism and Common Couple Violence: Two Forms of Violence against Women," *Journal of Marriage and the Family* 57 (May 1995), 284.

10. Robert L. Hampton and Richard J. Gelles, "A Profile of Violence toward Black Children," in Robert L. Hampton, ed., *Black Family Violence: Current Research and Theory* (Lexington, MA: D.C. Heath & Company, 1991), 33.

11. Ibid.

12. Manthia Diawara, ed., *Black American Cinema* (New York: Routledge, 1993), 11.

13. Valerie Smith, "Telling Family Secrets: Narrative Ideology in *Suzanne, Suzanne* by Camille Billops and James V. Hatch," in Diane Carson, Linda Dittmar, and Janice R. Welsch, eds., *Multiple Voices in Feminist Film Criticism* (Minneapolis: University of Minnesota Press, 1994), 388.

14. Nancy J. Haflin and Edna G. Bay, *Women in Africa: Studies in Social and Economic Change* (Palo Alto: Stanford University Press, 1976), 9.

15. Manthia Diawara, *African Film: Politics and Culture* (Bloomington: Indiana University Press, 1992), 144.

16. Deborah Fahy Bryceson, "Women's Proletarianization and the Family Wage in Tanzania," in Haleh Afshar, ed., *Women, Work, and Ideology in the Third World* (New York: Tavistock Publications, 1985), 128.

17. Ibid., 150.

18. Jenny Hammond, *Sweeter than Honey: Testimonies of Tigrayan Women* (Oxford: Third World First, 1989), 11.

19. Florence C. Ladd, "Sidet: Forced Exile," *Sage* 7, no. 1 (Summer 1990), 64.

20. Margaret Tiberio, "An Interview with Salem Mekuria," *Visions* (Winter 1991), 16.

21. Bill Nichols, *Representing Reality: Issues and Concepts in Documentary* (Bloomington: Indiana University Press, 1991), 181.

22. Cheryl Johnson-Odim, "Common Themes, Different Contexts: Third World Women and Feminism," in Chandra Talpade, Ann Russo, and Lourdes Torres, eds., *Third World Women and the Politics of Feminism* (Bloomington: Indiana University Press, 1991), 320.

———— 5 ————

Bugles, Bandoliers, and Body Bags: The Soldier's Saga through Film

John P. Lovell

War[1] has several features that give it a special character as a form of social conflict: (1) it is violence organized for political purposes, initiated by the political elites who head a sovereign state or insurgent or secessionist group; (2) the war typically is described to the populace as essential in order to deal with threats to community interests, certainly preferable to inaction or surrender. In other words, there are (except in the view of total pacifists) "good wars," "just wars,"[2] as well as "bad wars" and "unjust wars"; (3) entire societies have been mobilized and mass armies deployed in modern war; (4) for those given the responsibility of facing death on behalf of the state as soldiers,[3] the combat experience is an important rite of passage in the coming-of-age process; (5) the *way wars* are fought and their outcome reflect not only differences in tangible resources such as weaponry, but also intangible elements such as differences in political culture; (6) advanced industrial powers have tended to place a premium on technological dominance in warfare; (7) the dismal record of carnage and destruction resulting from twentieth-century warfare, coupled with the capabilities that have been developed to bring an end to civilization in a future war, have fostered diverse responses by governments, international organizations, and others. They also have been the inspiration for some of the most thought-provoking films on war as madness.

This discussion focuses primarily on feature films, rather than documentaries, most of them American (i.e., Hollywood) rather than foreign. Several exceptions to these generalizations are included, however, in order to illustrate a range of possibilities for films that can enhance instruction, particularly if one recognizes the creative possibilities for showing film excerpts rather than invariably showing films in their entirety. Given audiences consisting mainly of young (i.e., postadolescent) men and women, the plot lines of most of the films trace the saga of the soldier in time of war. Several of them have the additional merit (from my perspective) of capturing the irony, even the absurdity, of the human predicament as it is experienced in war.

The pool of motion pictures that could be recommended is considerably larger than the set of films discussed. However, not all—or even most—films about war "pass muster" for our needs. On the contrary, it is probably accurate to say that most "war films" romanticize acts of violence. Hollywood has produced some 450 "war films" since the end of World War II, 280 of these dealing with that war.[4] As noted in a guide to over 400 war movies now available on videocassette, "the war films made between 1930 and the mid-1960s generally present a view of war that is romantic, exciting, and heroic."[5] Simplistic plots portraying "good guys" overcoming adversity in their struggle against "bad guys" tend to gloss over political, strategic, technological, social, and moral complexities and nuances that may be essential to an in-depth understanding of actions and motives.

Still, just as one must guard against overgeneralizing about war, one ought not dismiss war movies out of hand on the basis of the deficiencies that have been especially conspicuous. Rather, the appropriate caveats are to have a clear idea of the purposes to be served in showing a film (or a portion thereof) and to review carefully the film before it is shown to be sure it will serve the intended purposes. Just because a movie gets a "four-star" rating in a widely distributed film guide does not mean that it will be helpful in illuminating those particular issues about the war upon which you, as instructor or discussion leader, wish to focus. Conversely, one might well find that a film that according to some criteria is quite mediocre (e.g., on someone's "two-star" list) will serve particular purposes well.

Criteria for film selection (with a personal illustration of each in parentheses) might well include: (1) the nature of the task at hand (e.g., teaching at a midwestern state university); (2) the intended audience (upper-level undergraduates and graduates, most of them American and mostly majoring in political science); (3) training and experience of the discussion leader (service in the U.S. armed forces followed by postgraduate study of political science, with more than thirty years of teaching and research on germane topics); (4) the issues being examined (courses in international relations dealing with international conflict, or with U.S. national security); (5) any special pedagogical contributions that the discussion leader hopes to make with these films (conveying a sense of irony, for instance).

Film can provide a powerful source of the vicarious experience of war. Particularly by getting the audience to identify with those caught up in war, films of the sort discussed in this chapter can illuminate important issues associated with various features of war identified in earlier discussion, guiding exploration beyond textbook cliches and homilies.

ORGANIZING VIOLENCE: "GOOD WARS" AND "BAD WARS"

Modern warfare has the potential for violence on a very large scale. Ironically, the growth to doomsday proportions of modern warfare is traceable not only to increases in the lethality of weaponry but also to the "democratization of war." The notion that "every citizen must be a soldier, and every soldier a citizen," which provided the rationale for the introduction of the *levée en masse* in the French Revolution, drew upon an ideal of civic obligation rooted in the militia system of the American colonies and tapped during the American war of independence.[6] In contrast to the practice that had prevailed for centuries, the American and the French revolutions mark the beginning of the modern era of patriotic appeals to the masses in time of war.

Nationalism and the appeals to patriotism, which were first evident during the American and French revolutions, led inexorably, beginning with the Napoleonic wars, to wars of mass mobilization. Simultaneously, warfare was becoming more "scientific," its planning and execution entrusted to specialists—professional soldiers, rather than amateurs as in the past. The Napoleonic wars, for example, became the focal point for one of the most influential books on the subject ever written, *On War*, by a Prussian, Karl von Clausewitz.[7] Paradoxically, modern warfare has become both democratized and professionalized.[8]

The contagious nature of the rhetoric and the acts that instigated the American and French revolutions unleashed a flood of movements for independence from colonial rule throughout the Western Hemisphere in the early nineteenth century; and then, in the twentieth century, in the Middle East and North Africa, Asia, and—in a torrent in the early 1960s—in sub-Saharan Africa.

From among many films, documentary as well as feature, that might be selected dealing with issues stemming from the violence of independence struggles, we limit our discussion to two. A British film *Gandhi* is an interesting place to start. Produced and directed by Richard Attenborough, the film stars Ben Kingsley in the title role, for which he received an Oscar in the 1982 Academy Awards ceremony—one of eight Oscars the film won. Gandhi's commitment to nonviolence is shown to be rooted not only in his sense of morality but also because he believed that this strategy would work. Given his understanding of British culture, he was convinced that, in time, the British would be shamed into granting independence to India. The film shows many tests of this proposition that nonviolence was the way to go throughout Gandhi's lifetime—not all of them convincing to fellow Indians. Then, the civil war that erupted when independence came raised still another question. Did Gandhi bear some responsibility for the awful bloodshed? One might want to select relevant segments from the total running time of three hours, given the focus of much of the film only indirectly, if at all, on these questions and issues.

Whereas the film *Gandhi* has a cast overflowing with well-known actors (e.g., John Gielgud, Geraldine James, Edward Fox, Candice Bergen, Trevor Howard, John Mills, and Martin Sheen), *The Battle of Algiers* earned its reputation for realism by eschewing professional actors in favor of locals on location in Algeria. Only Jean Martin, in the role of the French paratrooper-colonel who commands the counterrevolutionary operation, is a professional actor. Selected as the best film in film festivals in Venice in 1966 and New York in 1967, *The Battle of Algiers* depicts the ultimately successful struggle for independence from France of the FLN (Algerian National Liberation Front). From the opening scene of torture and interrogation of a FLN leader by a French officer to subsequent scenes of revolutionary violence, the film recalls the familiar observation that "one person's 'freedom fighter' is another person's 'terrorist.' " Stated somewhat differently, the film can provoke some useful discussion about arguments made to justify a strategy of violence—or non-violence—in pursuit of freedom from colonial rule.

Circumstances or contingencies under which the resort to war might be popular include not only acts of rebellion or revolution against colonial rule or a tyrannical regime. Rather, the use of armed force may seem essential to the preservation of the nation's territorial integrity and population from foreign aggression. World War II was such an occasion, in the minds of the overwhelming majority of allied populations. It was, in popular view, a "good war."[9]

MASS MOBILIZATION FOR WAR

The British model of a society-under-arms mobilized in support of the proposition that their government was waging a "good war" was helpful to President Franklin Roosevelt's efforts to rally the American public behind the war effort. The motion pictures being produced in Hollywood became an important resource to utilize toward this goal. An MGM production, *Mrs. Miniver*, was one of the most popular of its time in the United States. *Mrs. Miniver* was the winner of seven Academy Awards, including Best Picture of 1942, Best Actress (Greer Garson), and Best Supporting Actress (Teresa Wright). Walter Pidgeon was nominated for his role as Mrs. Miniver's husband, Clem, but the Best Actor award was given to James Cagney for his lead role in the patriotic film that was selected as Best Musical of the year, *Yankee Doodle Dandy*.

Garson, in the title role, played Kay Miniver, a woman whose good humor, determination, and ingenuity gave strength to others under difficult wartime conditions, especially German bombing raids. In the aftermath of one of the more devastating raids, a rousing speech by a vicar whose church was now rubble is exemplary of the societal mobilization theme. Essentially, his message was "This war is the responsibility of all of us, not just the soldiers in uniform." Winston Churchill, the British wartime leader who personified the gritty determination that would sustain the British through their darkest hour, said, after viewing *Mrs. Miniver,* that the movie was worth more than six divisions of troops.[10]

It is doubtful that Churchill would have had a similar reaction to another MGM movie set in England during World War II but not released until 1964. Indeed, it is inconceivable that *The Americanization of Emily* would have been produced or shown either in the United States or in Great Britain during World War II. Whereas *Mrs. Miniver* provides support for the notion of patriotic effort in a "good war," *The Americanization of Emily* ridicules and rejects such ideas. A lively and useful discussion can be stimulated by showing both films.

Paddy Chayefsky directed and wrote the screenplay for *The Americanization of Emily*, based on a novel of the same name by William Bradford Huie. The film features James Garner in the antihero role of U.S. Navy Lieutenant Charles E. Madison and Julie Andrews in a nonsinging role as Emily Barham. Madison's boss, Admiral William Jessup (Melvin Douglas), is involved in the preparations for the forthcoming channel crossing and D-Day invasion. Madison's assignment is to procure plenty of the various items, such as beer, whiskey, good cuts of beef, poker chips, and female companions that will keep the admiral and other "brass" happy. When Madison approaches Emily, a WAAF driver, to try to recruit her for an evening card game with the admiral and some of his cronies, she rejects the overture with righteous indignation. Her reversal of that decision, after being scornfully rebuked by one of her WAAF colleagues, breaks the ice; but her relationship with Madison experiences other chills and thaws during the remainder of the film.

Madison is startled when his admiral comes up with an idea of how to ensure that Congress will look favorably on the navy. "The first dead man on Omaha Beach must be a sailor!" the admiral tells Madison, with the instruction to arrange for the filming of the event. Much against his better judgment, but prompted, finally at gunpoint, by his zealous coworker, Lieutenant Commander "Bus" Cummings (James Coburn), Charlie finds himself with the sailor-photographer (Keenan Wynn) participating in the invasion. Happily for Charlie, and for the movie audience, Emily has become "Americanized" by now and helps Charlie narrowly avert the fate of becoming the literal fulfillment of a crazy admiral's order.

The Americanization of Emily takes potshots at the notion, implicit in most previous films on World War II, such as *Mrs. Miniver*, that it was a "good war" deserving of full support from the American (British, etc.) people. Charlie articulates a very different point of view in a conversation with Emily's mother (played by Joyce Grenfell):

Wars are always fought for the best of reasons. . . . So far this war we've managed to butcher some ten million humans in the interest of humanity. . . . It's not war that's unnatural with us; it's virtue. As long as valor remains a virtue we shall have soldiers. So I preach cowardice. Through cowardice we shall be saved.

One may disagree with Charlie's apparent embrace of cowardice and still find it helpful to an assessment of the "good" World War II to be reminded, as George Kennan has written, that it really was a continuation, after a twenty-year's truce, of the "bad" first world war:

[World War II] developed and rolled its course with the relentless logic of the last act of a classical tragedy. And the main elements of that tragic situation—the sickness and impatience of Germany, the weakness of Eastern Europe, the phenomenon of Bolshevism in Russia, and the weariness and debility in France and England—all these things took their origin so clearly in the period of 1914–1920 that it seems to be here, if anywhere, that the real answers should be sought.[11]

None of the European governments that called their societies to arms in 1914 had anticipated that the war would drag on for four years; nor had the masses, when asked to rally to their nation's cause. When the German kaiser told his armed forces at the beginning of the war that they would be back home "before the leaves have fallen from the trees," there is little doubt that he was appealing to a receptive audience, who were ready to fight for their fatherland with the expectation of a quick success.[12]

However, four years of trench warfare took an enormous toll in carnage and in morale. The painful transformation in attitude, which took place among soldiers at the front before it affected civilians in their homes, is vividly portrayed in the film classic *All Quiet on the Western Front*. American reviewers generally praised Director Lewis Milestone for the American-produced motion picture, filmed on ranch land in California. At the Academy Awards ceremony, he was named Best Director and *All Quiet* was named the Best Motion Picture of 1930. The antiwar message of both the film and the German novel by Erich Maria Remarque on which the film script was based made them controversial, however. The author of a study of the twentieth century struggles of the American peace movement describes the English translation of *All Quiet on the Western Front* as "the most popular war story in America." Its portrayal of the "gory and senseless slaughter" of World War I helped foster the "never again" sentiment that President Franklin Roosevelt would find difficult to overcome.[13] Official measures to ban the film and novel were taken not only in Germany after Hitler and the Nazis came to power, but also in Britain and France, their leaders fearful of the consequences if the citizenry should become unduly pacific.

The disenchantment with World War I was also the inspiration for a much more recent (1981) but powerful Australian film, *Gallipoli*. The Gallipoli peninsula, adjacent to the straits of the Dardanelles, is the site of a military campaign that was conducted under British auspices in 1915. The supply routes to Britain's Russian allies through the Dardanelles had become vulnerable to attack when Turkey entered the war on the side of Germany. The goal of the Gallipoli campaign was to secure the routes; it proved to be such a dismal failure, however, that First Lord of the Admiralty, Winston Churchill, was ousted and would look back on the events as the low point in his career.

The Gallipoli campaign is largely ignored in American history textbooks, which focus instead on the battles in France where American troops would see action three years later. In Australia, the campaign has historical importance, marked with an annual holiday. Thousands of Australian volunteers died serving under British overall command with the ANZAC (Australia–New Zealand) force in a futile attack on entrenched Turkish positions, designed to decoy the enemy from the British main thrust.

As the film *Gallipoli* is vague about the strategic and historic details, an instructor showing it would be advised to provide them for students. This defect aside, *Gallipoli* has much to recommend it. Screening it in tandem with *All Quiet* can highlight some differences, as well as similarities, in the experience of war, which, in turn, can provide a basis for discussing some valuable lessons.

Viewing both films helps one to recognize that one's generalizations about war need to be tempered with the recognition of the many sources of diversity of the experience, which shape the soldier's perspective. The battle in the Gallipoli Peninsula was a different war from that being waged on the Western Front. Trench warfare on both fronts in World War I was different from that experienced in the more fast-moving battles of World War II. Even within World War II, war in Europe differed from jungle warfare in the Pacific. Ground combat differed from the air war, which, in turn, was different from the war at sea, or under the sea.

More recently, Vietnam was a different war for Americans than it was for either America's Vietnamese adversary or the Vietnamese allies. (Failure fully to recognize this elementary point was part of the cultural misperception that would become a fatal flaw in U.S. policy, as will be discussed shortly.) For the American soldier, the war in Vietnam obviously was an experience different in important respects from the war in Korea, and both, in turn, differed somewhat from the World War II experiences. Even those who shared the experience of having served in Vietnam "during the war" are likely to have differing perspectives depending upon variables such as the year in which he or she served, the arm of service and type unit, and whether the assignment was in Saigon or out in "the boonies."

Moreover, whereas civilian politicians and bureaucrats and military "brass" might find a logic and order to events, an ordinary soldier (a Paul Baumer in *All Quiet*, an Archy Hamilton or a Frank Dunne in *Gallipoli*) sees little but disorder from his vantage point. As John Keegan has noted:

Battle, for [the front-line soldier] takes place in a wildly unstable physical and emotional environment; he may spend much of his time in combat as a mildly apprehensive spectator, granted, by some freak of events, a comparatively danger-free grandstand view of others fighting; then he may suddenly be able to see nothing but the clods on which he has flung himself for safety, there to crouch—he cannot anticipate—for minutes or for hours; he may feel in turn boredom, exultation, panic, anger, sorrow, bewilderment, even that sublime emotion we call courage.[14]

COMBAT AS A RITE OF PASSAGE

Courage is not only a "sublime emotion" but a quality that is central to understanding the meaning of war for the soldier. Wars are fought disproportionately by the young—post-adolescents seeking to establish their individual identity at the same time that proving they are worthy of being accepted by their peers assumes importance. In both *All Quiet on the Western Front* and *Gallipoli,* the central characters are young soldiers. Paul Baumer (played by Lew Ayres) is depicted in *All Quiet* as just a German schoolboy when the war begins, who with several of his schoolmates is encouraged by the schoolmaster to enlist in the army. The progressive loss of innocence, once the young soldiers must confront the realities of survival in battle, culminates for Paul in a return home on leave. He pays a visit to his old school, where the schoolmaster asks him to share with the students some of the valuable lessons he has learned as a soldier. To the dismay of his schoolmaster, his description of war to the students emphasizes the horrors rather than patriotism or duty.

The Australian film *Gallipoli*, directed by Peter Weir, focuses on the adventures and travails of two young men whose initial encounter is as competitors in a running meet in Western Australia. Both respond enthusiastically to the appeal by a visiting military delegation from the Light Horse Regiment. When eighteen-year-old Archie Hamilton (played by Mark Lee) is turned away as being too young, Frank Dunne (Mel Gibson), a few years older, persuades him to go across Australia to Perth to enlist. The film follows the two on a trek across the Australian desert to some difficult moments getting accepted in the military, then to a staging area for the ANZAC operation in Egypt, and finally to the denouement on the battlefield for which the film is named.

That it has taken roughly an hour and a half of the approximately two-hour running time of the film to get to actual battle has led one reviewer to protest that "it would be incorrect to call *Gallipoli* an antiwar film."[15] To be sure, the percentage of time in which the principals are in battle is much lower in *Gallipoli* than in *All Quiet*, for example. On the other hand, a poignant implicit theme of this book is one of "shattered dreams," which is illustrated forcefully by the death of Archy, whom we have come to know in his full enthusiastic embrace of life, just as it is in Paul's death, his dreams already worn down by months in the trenches. Peter Weir, who wrote the script and directed the film, puts the Archie-Frank saga in a larger context that helps to explain it.

It took us a great deal of research...to realize that we did lose our own flower of a nation. . . . A special kind of man went. Sure, they were adventurers, but a very simple kind. They weren't bloodthirsty swashbucklers, but they were a kind of warrior class. . . . Two hundred and fifty thousand of them went away, and, in a sense, none of them ever came back. . . . not the same men.[16]

In short, both films provide vivid illustrations of a coming-of-age process that is accelerated by war. Combat takes on the characteristics of a rite of passage. The young soldier's eagerness to prove his mettle as a warrior gives way to disillusionment, as death and destruction become part of his routine. Yet, as both films illustrate and research findings document, a sense of comradeship develops among those with whom the soldier shares the combat experience.

Ties to comrades-in-arms were a crucial source of support and motivation for American soldiers during World War II, for example, according to attitude surveys conducted by Samuel Stouffer and a large team of associates. Their research also revealed that patriotism, while not irrelevant, tended to be an uncomfortable abstraction for the soldier.[17] Wartime studies of the sources of cohesion or disintegration of German army units also found that primary group ties rather than a more abstract sense of patriotism are important to a soldier in combat.[18]

To emphasize the importance of emotional ties to one's comrades-in-arms as an element of combat motivation is not to say that soldiers thrown together by the fortunes of war into a common combat unit will invariably form a cohesive whole. For the American soldier in Vietnam, fragile bonds of group cohesion were subjected to stress by factors such as a rapid turnover of personnel and, in the later stages of the war, highly publicized antiwar protests in the home front. Thus, it is not surprising that in many cases soldiers adopted an attitude that largely denied obligations to the group when these conflicted with the primary concern for "taking care of number one."[19]

BODY COUNTS AND SORTIES: HIGH-TECH AMERICA AT WAR IN VIETNAM

By now, there are dozens of highly rated feature films that provide insight into the American experience in Vietnam. The motion picture industry, consistent with the public mood and in company with television and governmental institutions (including the armed forces), had tried to forget about Vietnam.[20] There had been a virtual moratorium on films on the subject since the painful televised spectacle of American helicopters fleeing Saigon in 1975. Oliver Stone's *Platoon,* selected for an Oscar as Best Picture of 1987, was an important signal of change. Stone's experience as an infantryman in Vietnam gives the film authenticity both in the dialogue and in visual effects. Stone won an Oscar as Best Director and was nominated for Best Screenplay.

Two other interesting feature films based on actual experience in Vietnam are *Good Morning, Vietnam,* released in 1987, and *Born on the Fourth of July,* a 1989 release. The film's title, *Good Morning, Vietnam,* is the way disc jockey Adrian Cronauer (played by Robin Williams) signed on daily in his broadcasts for the U.S. Armed Forces Radio in Saigon. Although the film lacks the impact of *Platoon*, Williams's comedic genius gives it a "MASH"-like quality of commentary on war and the institutions that perpetuate it.

Born on the Fourth of July depicts the transition of Ron Kovic (played by Tom Cruise) from fierce combat in Vietnam, where he became a much decorated hero (with a birth date to match) and also a paraplegic, to the antiwar demonstrations in the States, which he joined as an angry activist.

The strength of these films is also their limitation. In the hands of a talented director, a story that is developed around the actual experience of a soldier and his comrades-in-arms can be an effective way to elicit audience identification with the soldier. However, with regard to the war in Vietnam, typically the instructor has additional goals. These are likely to include some concern with explaining how and why the United States became involved in Vietnam, why the seemingly stronger party in the war did not prevail (how could a superpower like the United States possibly lose?), and why the involvement became so divisive among Americans.

For exploration of these questions, my strong recommendation is not a feature film, but *Hearts and Minds*, which is, technically, a documentary as it contains real footage of real people expressing their thoughts, rather than actors reading scripts. Coproduced by Peter Davis, who also directed it, and Bert Schneider, *Hearts and Minds* combines footage from newscasts with interviews into a powerful indictment of the American involvement in Vietnam. It became the object of heated reviews when released, critics on the political Right seeing it as "anti-American" and "manipulative"; critics on the Left complaining that the filmmakers hedged and were unduly sympathetic to American policymakers.

The film certainly is not flawless; there are several scenes that, in my judgment, are of dubious merit and could be shortened if not eliminated entirely (as I have done when less time was available than the two-hour running time). Moreover, this film could fit the description of its harshest critics if it is shown without ensuring that the audience has acquired a good working knowledge of the key events, actions, and policies. Preparing the audience is especially important; that accomplished, there is much to gain.

Hearts and Minds reminds us (or should) that the U.S. government, like all governments, has an enormous capacity for self-deception, as well as a capacity to employ slogans and arguments designed to manipulate support for war policies of dubious quality at best. As an "angry" documentary, *Hearts and Minds* is valuable in providing insight into the sense of outrage that became widespread among Americans in the 1970s. The flimsy rationale for the escalating involvement is seen. President Eisenhower solemnly explains the "domino effect" that would be set in motion if the United States should abandon its South Vietnamese ally. President Lyndon Johnson, under whom the U.S. involvement changed from an advisory capacity to the commitment of full units of American armed forces, gives a speech that underscores the title of the film: "The ultimate victory will be winning the hearts and minds of the people who actually live out there."

Other major participants in shaping the policies over the years are seen and heard in the film. Some of the most illuminating of these are persons who, in retrospect, think the policies pursued by the United States were ill-advised. Clark Clifford, for instance, had been solidly supportive of continuing the U.S. involvement in Vietnam when asked by President Lyndon Johnson to take over as secretary of defense. Robert McNamara, one of the "best and the brightest" core of top advisers that John Kennedy had assembled upon becoming president, had been a zealous devotee of the counterinsurgency strategy in Vietnam. Grown disillusioned, however, he was moving on from the Pentagon to head the World Bank.[21] Clifford's first major task as secretary of defense was that of assessing a request from General Westmoreland for 206,000 more American troops to be sent to Vietnam, in the wake of the Tet offensive, a surprise attack on the Vietnamese New Year's holiday by North Vietnamese regular forces in collaboration with Viet Cong guerrillas. The attacking forces had failed to topple the South Vietnamese regime; but they had struck as far as inside the wall of the United States embassy in Saigon and had made assaults on more than a hundred other locations throughout South Vietnam. Clifford's review of the situation led him to the conclusion that to put additional American forces in Vietnam, as General Westmoreland requested, supported by the joint chiefs of staff, would be to compound error. He is remarkably forthright in admitting to his interviewer: "I was wrong! We were wrong!"

Moreover, J. William Fulbright, who held an important position as chairman of the Senate Foreign Relations Committee, says in an interview that President Johnson and other officials have lied to the American people about the reasons American forces are needed. "A lie is a lie," Fulbright says, making precisely the point that led to the "credibility gap," a profound distrust in government on the part of Americans.

The value of *Hearts and Minds* is most evident, it seems to me, when one recognizes that the film is really about the clash of cultures. The conflicts generated by the presence in the traditional culture of Vietnam of armed representatives of a foreign culture and the susceptibility of the situation to cultural misperception are skillfully demonstrated in *Hearts and Minds* through juxtaposing scenes in ways that make commentary unnecessary. For example, there is a burial scene in Vietnam in which a young boy is crying, clutching a framed portrait of a soldier, presumably his father. An older woman—mother of the deceased soldier, one surmises—also is weeping loudly and even attempts to crawl into the grave when the casket is lowered. The screen then changes to a shot of the commander of all American ground forces in Vietnam, General William Westmoreland, explaining, "The Oriental doesn't place the value on human life that we do."

Moreover, *Hearts and Minds* is valuable in demonstrating that the Vietnam War had many victims—not just soldiers killed in battle. Some of the most powerful moments in the film are those with footage of American military personnel in lesser roles and interviews conducted not only with some of the individuals who were in positions to influence policy but those in more humble assignments. There is a naval aviator, Lieutenant George Coker, for instance, whom we see first being welcomed back to his hometown in New Jersey after spending months as a prisoner of war in North Vietnam. Later, there is a scene of him talking to a group of women, explaining that it was images of "good old mom" and how she might react that had sustained the American POWs. Then, introduced by a nun to a classroom of children, Coker explains that it has been a long war; but we went there to win and we did. Asked by a student what Vietnam is like, he tells them that it would be a beautiful country except for the people, who make a mess of things.

However, interviews with another man who flew sorties over Vietnam, Randy Floyd, reveal a very different reaction to the experience. The effect is magnified by the editing technique of showing different segments at different parts of the film, creating a progression in audience understanding of Floyd's views that matches the progression of the transformation that has occurred in his outlook. Thus, the early clip has him describing the satisfaction one gets of flying a bombing mission when it is well executed. It is only later that he discusses the inhumane nature of the mission, with antipersonnel bombs designed to tear to shreds anyone in the target area, sometimes leaving victims alive but in terrible pain. Because he was flying several thousand feet above where the bombs landed, he could not hear the screams of victims, he observes remorsefully. Nor could he see them. "I don't know what I'd do if my children were exposed to this," he says. There is a painful pause. Floyd is unable to speak. Then he observes that he can't even cry, because his macho upbringing has precluded it.

Several other interviewees have stories to tell or things to say that provide insight into American culture and the diversity of reactions to the war: Edward Sowders, an Army deserter who has decided to give himself up, is shown talking nervously with his equally nervous mother prior to testifying before a nationally congressional committee hearing. Robert Muller describes the emotional pain that he, once a proud Marine Corps lieutenant, now a wheelchair-bound paraplegic, experienced attending a Marine Corps ceremony. David and Mary Emerson are interviewed in their home in Concord, Massachusetts, as they reminisce about their Harvard graduate son who was killed in Vietnam. And there is William Marshall, whose graphic street talk adds both gallows humor and insight. He describes being caught in the artillery barrage with a body blown on top of him, "napalm drippin' all over him, you dig?" The early shots of Marshall are from the waist up; it is only near the end of the film that the screen reveals that Marshall has lost his legs in the war. It is here that he says people are trying to forget about the war, but he isn't going to let you forget. "Dig?"

LEARNING TO STOP WORRYING AND. . .

Among the facets of American political culture highlighted by *Hearts and Minds* is a bias that equates "can-do" with "ought-to-do," as reflected in an extravagant reliance on high-tech weaponry to fight wars. Several references during the film to the death and devastation in Vietnam wrought by American bombing are illustrative. Perhaps the classic symbol is the B-52, the heavy bomber that was the pride of the Strategic Air Command (SAC) for many years, which flew hundreds of sorties to targets in Vietnam from Guam and from Thailand. From the initiation of Operation "Rolling Thunder" in 1965 until the Paris accords in 1973, the tonnage of bombs dropped by American planes in the air war in Southeast Asia was more than four times the amount American aircraft dropped in all of World War II. Although atomic bombs were not used in Vietnam, the "conventional" bombs that were dropped were the equivalent in explosive force to some 640 Hiroshimas.[22] And yet, the technological superpower lost the war.

The lessons of the war in Vietnam are shrouded in irony and paradox. Contrary to those who attribute the calamitous U.S. involvement to the malfunctioning of the intelligence apparatus, blunders in top-level decision making, poor communications, failures of congressional oversight, or some combination of such problems, Leslie Gelb and Richard Betts have shown that the American political system "worked" about as well as one ought to expect. Their point is not that the policies were well reasoned—or successful. They simply argue that "Vietnam was not an aberration of the decision making system but a logical culmination of the principles that leaders brought with them into it."[23]

Moreover, as Earl Ravenal has shown, despite the breakdown of consensus on foreign policy, which American presidents had enjoyed prior to the escalation of American involvement, in the aftermath of Vietnam there was virtual across-the-board agreement that the United States should "never again" get involved in another "Vietnam." The problem has been that "never again" means very different things to different people. For instance, to some it means "never again get into a war of type X," "X" being defined as "that we don't intend to win, using all necessary force"; whereas to others it is "never again get into a war that makes demands on resources needed for domestic programs." Ravenal argues convincingly that, in practice, the apparent restraint demonstrated by the widespread cries of "never again" does not augur well either for avoiding getting drawn into a morass in the future, or for forging a consensus on the circumstances under which it is appropriate for the United States to commit its armed forces.[24]

Despite the intensity of emotions generated by the American involvement in Vietnam, the war really made no significant difference on policies being pursued nor on the way American governmental institutions operated.[25] At first blush, one may be inclined to reject out of hand this assertion, the conclusion drawn by the editors of a major review of the war's impact by experts in various fields. The argument is not that the war was ignored by the American government and society, nor that it was just a routine event. Rather, much as Gelb and Betts argue that "the system worked" to produce the policy decisions that defined the pattern of escalating U.S. involvement, Osborn, et al., find from the review of policies and institutions that had been conducted ten years after the last American helicopter had left Saigon (Ho Chi Minh City), that the changes triggered by the war were more superficial than basic; fundamentally not much had changed.

Many inferences might be drawn from these various assessments. Speculation on alternatives may be enhanced by a provocative satirical film from the mid-1960s, *Doctor Strangelove: or, How I Learned to Stop Worrying and Love the Bomb*. Produced and directed by Stanley Kubrick, who also wrote the screenplay, and based on the novel *Red Alert*, by Peter George, *Dr. Strangelove* recaptures the Cold War context that had long shaped discussions of war and peace in the United States. To appreciate the film fully, therefore, it is necessary to have familiarity with some of the basic elements of deterrence theory that were at the core of the Cold War "mind set," as well as with some of the key characters.

In 1953, the year Dwight D. Eisenhower took over the presidency from Harry Truman, the Soviet Union successfully tested a hydrogen bomb. Their successful test of an atomic bomb in 1949 had come earlier than most American experts had predicted. Acquisition now of an H-bomb was evidence of a growing military and scientific capability that, it was feared, would embolden the Soviets to continue the "master plan" of Communist expansion. In order to convince the Soviets that the costs to them of any such aggression would exceed any possible benefits, the Eisenhower administration announced a doctrine of "massive retaliation." Simply put, the Soviets were put on notice that any aggression by them in any part of the world would be responded to, not necessarily by a dispatch of troops to the scene, but rather "massively—by means, and at places, of our choosing." Implicitly, the threat put Moscow at risk of nuclear attack if the Soviets took any action that threatened American vital interests.

In order for the threat of "massive retaliation" to be effective, however, it had to be believable—"credible deterrence" was the key. The centerpiece of the American deterrence strategy was the Strategic Air Command (SAC), with its heavy jet aircraft capable of carrying two atomic bombs each to targets in Soviet territory as distant as 1300 miles from their widely dispersed home bases, if refueled in-flight. At any one time, 24 hours a day, several dozen SAC bombers would be airborne, flying toward their targets until they reached a "fail-safe" point. Then they would turn and head home, unless the decision had been made at the highest levels of government to go to war. In that extreme case, a coded message would be received by each plane ordering it to proceed to its assigned target.

General Curtis LeMay, a cigar-chomping, no-nonsense taskmaster, who was an outspoken advocate of strategic bombing as the key to victory in war, surely influenced the creation of Kubrick's generals, Jack D. Ripper (Sterling Hayden) and "Buck" Turgidson (George C. Scott) As colorful (and, to some, as frightening) a character as either of them, LeMay had gained fame in World War II as the energetic, hard-bitten aviator who masterminded and led the bombing raids on Tokyo, which resulted in devastating firestorms. Placed in command of the Strategic Air Command in 1948, he presided over a dramatic increase in SAC's personnel, aircraft, and budget. He was chief of staff of the Air Force at the time of the most dramatic escalation of American involvement under Lyndon Johnson.

A possible model for Kubrick's Strangelove (one of three roles played by Peter Sellers) was Herman Kahn, a major Cold War guru. Trained as a physicist, Kahn had been at RAND, the most influential "think tank" for strategic concerns in the early post–World War II era. Kahn left RAND to found his own think tank, the Hudson Institute. In one of his early major works, *On Thermonuclear War*, Kahn develops scenarios that lead the reader through world wars 3 through 8 and describes a "doomsday machine" as embodying the ultimate logic of deterrence.

Another character that undoubtedly influenced Sellers's portrayal, under Kubrick's direction, of the Dr. Strangelove character, was Wernher von Braun, the head of America's space program. During World War II, von Braun had headed the German V-2 rocket program at Peenemunde. Near the end of the war, von Braun arranged to surrender his team to the Americans rather than fall into the hands of the Soviets. The irony of entrusting the American effort to prevail in the space race to scientists who had been in the employ of the Nazis, was not lost on humorists of the day.

Dr. Strangelove begins with *Leper Colony*, a B-52 under the command of Major King Kong (played by "Slim" Pickens) approaching its fail-safe point. Next, at SAC's Burpelson Air Force Base, the commanding officer, General Jack D. Ripper (Sterling Hayden), is explaining to his polite but incredulous operations officer, Group-Captain Lionel Mandrake (one of Peter Sellers's three roles) why it looks like global war has started with "the commies." He is putting his base on Condition Red, sealing off the base and ordering Mandrake to send the Go-code to the B-52s.

The scene then flashes to Washington, D.C., where the chairman of the Joint Chiefs of Staff, General "Buck" Turgidson (George C. Scott) gets a phone call telling him that monitoring of transmissions coming from Burpelson Air Base has revealed that an attack order has been sent to the B-52 wing on patrol; furthermore, all efforts to communicate with Burpelson have failed. The American president, Merkin Muffley (Peter Sellers) calls an emergency meeting in the Pentagon of the National Security Council. A briefing on the situation by General Turgidson leads to questions by the president and a general discussion of how to avert disaster. Special attention is paid to the views of the expert consultant, Dr. Strangelove (Peter Sellers). The scene shifts back and forth among the three principal sites for the remainder of the film.

Zany details provide testimony to Kubrick's skillful satiric adaptation of Peter George's novel—the erotic symbolism of the in-flight refueling of a B-52 at the beginning of the film; the Orwellian use of language of peace/war; the co-pilot of *Leper Colony* admiring a *Playboy* centerfold in a *Foreign Affairs* cover; the lyrics of the ballad "We'll meet again, don't know where, don't know when" being sung as a mushroom cloud fills the screen ending the film.

Reviewers found it difficult to sort out their reactions to this film, although some common themes emerged. For instance, in a lengthy review in *Film Comment,* Stephen Taylor describes *Strangelove* as "a bad film" but one that is

a milestone. . . . [halting the customary] deification of the Air Force. . . . [hauling] the Tellers, Kahns, and Von Brauns out of the macabre shadows of technical omniscience into welcome . . . light of totally sarcastic scrutiny. . . . [bringing] to the screen an idea that [we have long shared:] that *we may have entrusted our survival to a bevy of screwballs.* . . . [However,] the wit and elegance of Moliere or Swift are replaced by comic anarchy.[26]

Similarly, Bosley Crowther, in the *New York Times*, expresses his dismay at the "brazenly jesting speculation of what might happen [in a nuclear crisis] within...the most responsible council of the President." Nevertheless,

Crowther finds the film "at the same time one of the cleverest and most incisive satiric thrusts at the awkwardness and folly of the military that have ever been on the screen." However, he is still puzzled. "When *virtually everybody turns up stupid or insane*—or, what is worse, psychotic—I want to know what this picture proves," Crowther complains.[27]

A review of *Dr. Strangelove* by Tom Milne in *Sight and Sound*, in effect answers Crowther's question: "*Everybody, one realizes by the end, is mad. And Kubrick's frightening vision here is the enormity of madness which can lie behind an exterior sane enough to walk, talk, and work with calm competence, or behind a perfectly reasonable remark.*"[28]

One might conclude, with Rousseau, that "To be sane in a world of madmen is in itself a kind of madness." This realization provides a fitting conclusion to a discussion of films about war.[29]

NOTES

1. In everyday parlance, "war" is a term used to describe a wide array of social conflicts that erupt into violence—"rumbles" between rival urban street gangs, for instance; longstanding feuds between segments of the lumber industry and environmentalist groups over usage of national forests; even intramarital disputes (viz., the film *War of the Roses*). Without minimizing the intensity to which such conflicts can develop, it is useful for present purposes to apply the term more narrowly here—in accord with usage by theorists as well as practitioners in the field of international relations.

2. See Michael Walzer, *Just and Unjust Wars: A Moral Argument with Historical Illustrations*, 2d ed. (New York: Basic Books, 1992, 1977).

3. "Soldiers" is a term used throughout the essay as a shorthand expression to refer to men and women in all of the armed forces.

4. Data from "The Media and Images of War: Perception Versus Reality," *The Defense Monitor* 32 (1994), 3. The *Monitor* is a newsletter produced by the Center for Defense Information, an organization founded by a group of retired U.S. Navy officers in the early 1970s to serve as a self-designated "watchdog" over Pentagon activity and gather information and provide commentary essential to public consideration of alternatives to officially endorsed national security initiatives.

5. *War Movies* (Evanston, IL: CineBooks, 1989), vii.[No author or editor is listed.]

6. See Walter Millis, *Arms and Men: A Study of American Military History* (New York: G. P. Putnam's Sons; 1956; Mentor reprint 1958).

7. Clausewitz's influence on American military thinking has been revived in the aftermath of a deep sense of malaise after Vietnam. See Harry G. Summers,

Jr., *On Strategy II: A Critical Analysis of the Gulf War* (New York: Dell, 1992), especially 126–135.

8. Details of the "democratization of war" phenomenon, with special attention to the American context, are provided by Millis, *Arms and Men*, 11–63; and Eliot A. Cohen, *Citizens and Soldiers: The Dilemmas of Military Service* (Ithaca, NY: Cornell University Press, 1985), 42–86.

9. See Studs Terkel, *The Good War: An Oral History of World War II* (New York: Pantheon Books, 1954). For a philosophical discussion of the issue, see Walzer, *Just and Unjust Wars*.

10. *War Movies*, 105.

11. George F. Kennan, *American Diplomacy 1900–1950* (Chicago: University of Chicago Press, 1951; Mentor reprint 1952), 51.

12. Quoted in John G. Stoessinger, *Why Nations Go to War*, 6th ed. (New York: St. Martin's, 1993), 1.

13. Lawrence S. Wittner, *Rebels against War: The American Peace Movement, 1933–1983* rev. ed. (Philadelphia: Temple University Press, 1984) 1–2.

14. John Keegan, *The Face of Battle* (New York: Vintage Press, 1987), 47.

15. Karen Jaehne, review of *Gallipoli*, *Cineaste* 11, no. 4 (1982): 40–43.

16. Peter Weir, interviewed by Claudia and Peter Fonda-Bonardi, "The Birth of a Nation," *Cineaste* 11 no. 4 (1982): 41–42.

17. Samuel A. Stouffer, et al., *The American Soldier*, 4 vols. (Princeton, NJ: Princeton University Press, 1949).

18. See S.L.A.Marshall, *Men against Fire* (New York: William Morrow, 1947). Also Roger Little, "Buddy Relations and Combat Performance," in Morris Janowitz, ed., *The New Military: Changing Patterns of Organization* (New York: Russell Sage Foundation, 1964), 195–224; and Edward A. Shils and Morris Janowitz, "Cohesion and Disintegration in the Wehrmacht in World War II," *Public Opinion Quarterly* 12 (Summer 1962): 280–315.

19. Charles C. Moskos, Jr., "The American Combat Soldier in Vietnam," *Journal of Social Issues* 31, no. 4 (1975): 25–37. Also Lawrence M. Baskir and William A. Strauss, *Chance and Circumstance: The Draft, the War and the Vietnam Generation* (New York: Knopf 1978; reprint, Random House, Vintage Books, 1978), 150–53.

20. For an elaboration, see James William Gibson, *The Perfect War: The War We Couldn't Lose and How We Did* (New York: Atlantic Monthly Press, 1986; reprint Vintage Books, 1988), 3–8. Also relevant is John P. Lovell, "Vietnam and the U.S. Army: Learning to Cope with Failure," in George K. Osborn, et al., *Democracy, Strategy, and Vietnam* (Lexington, MA: Lexington Books, 1987), 121–54.

21. See David Halberstam, *The Best and the Brightest* (New York: Random House, 1971; reprint, Greenwich, CT: Fawcett, 1973).

22. The data are presented within the context of an extensive discussion of what the author, Gibson, describes as "technowar," in *The Perfect War*, especially

Part 3, 319–420, "Death from Above." See also Loren Baritz, *Backfire: American Culture and the Vietnam War* (New York: William Morrow; 1985; reprint Ballantine Books, 1986).

23. Leslie H. Gelb, with Richard K. Betts, *The Irony of Vietnam: The System Worked* (Washington, DC: Brookings Institution, 1979).

24. Earl C. Ravenal, *Never Again: Learning from America's Foreign Policy Failure* (Philadelphia: Temple University Press, 1978).

25. Osborn, et al., ed., *Democracy, Strategy, and Vietnam.*

26. Stephen Taylor, review of *Dr. Strangelove, Film Comment* 2, no. 1 (Winter 1964): 40–43. Emphasis is added.

27. Bosley Crowther, review of *Dr. Strangelove, New York Times*, Jan. 31, 1964. Emphasis is added.

28. Tom Milne, review of *Dr. Strangelove,* Sight and Sound 33, no. 1 (Winter 1963–1964) 37–38. Emphasis is added.

29. Sources consulted in addition to those previously cited include Richard J. Barnet, *The Rocket's Red Glare: War, Politics, and the American Presidency* (New York: Simon and Schuster, 1990); Paul Boyer, *By the Bomb's Early Light: American Thought and Culture at the Dawn of the Atomic Age* (New York: Pantheon Books, 1985); D'Ann Campbell, *Women at War with America: Private Lives in a Patriotic Era* (Cambridge, MA: Harvard University Press, 1984); Francesca M. Cancian and James William Gibson, *Making War, Making Peace: The Social Foundations of Violent Conflict* (Belmont, CA: Wadsworth, 1990); Freeman Dyson, *Weapons and Hope* (New York: Harper & Row, 1984; paperback reprint 1985); H. Bruce Franklin, *War Stars: The Superweapon and the American Imagination* (New York: Oxford University Press, 1988); Lawrence\Freedman, ed., *War* (New York: Oxford University Press, 1994); Paul Fussell, *The Great War and Modern Memory* (New York: Oxford University Press, 1975; paperback reprint 1977). We have scratched the surface of film possibilities. This essay on war neglects closely related topics such as films dealing with science fiction, terrorism, and survivalist cults.

Part II

Caveats

——— 6 ———

Making the Classroom a Safe Environment

Barbara Allen

On Sunday, August 13, 1960, the satellite Echo I, an early victory in the "space race" with the Soviet Union, signaled a national triumph in the Cold War as it twinkled across night skies. One of a number of productions in the Cold War repertory, "little echo" allowed American spectators to participate in the nation's statecraft, as families gathered in the evening to view the stagecraft responsible for democracy's symbolic victory over communism.

While the war for outer space that week brought celebration of U.S. technological superiority, competition for ideological space on terra firma occasioned national disgrace. On Wednesday, Air Force pilot Gary Francis Powers went on trial for espionage in the Soviet Union after his U-2 had been brought down during a clandestine reconnaissance mission. The United States faced trial in the world court of public opinion as spy and provocateur for a mission it repeatedly denied ordering. U.S. technology had failed to prevent discovery of this survey of enemy territory, an even more devastating abasement of national prestige.

Cold War space exploits involved more than monitoring the "enemy" or even the mythic scale of humanity's race to lay claim to the universe. An ideological war, with "military actions" for "containment," it depended on assembling a massive arsenal of nuclear weapons. Containment strategy demanded and delivered the anxiety of imminent danger from nuclear annihilation. From fact to fiction, media representations reinforced this psychic war of uncertainty. Threats that these weapons might actually be used were taken seriously enough that Americans prepared themselves by building fallout shelters in their homes and communities.

In my midwestern hometown of 5,500, many families did not wait for nuclear war to find protection from the enemy in a bomb shelter. Instead, they first used them from Tuesday, August 15, until Thursday, August 17, 1960, to keep their children safe during a two-day air and ground search by 500 people that turned up the body of my grade school friend Avril "Honey" Terry. The denouement of our quarantine in shelters appointed for security from foreign threat confirmed the worst fears of the anxious parents: my friend had been kidnapped, raped, murdered, and dismembered on her way to spend her birthday money at our local toy store. The confessed perpetrator of the crime, twice-convicted rapist Emmett Hashfield, was a 53–year-old toy maker with a record of sex offenses dating back more than 30 years. Events further inscribed my consciousness with the personal insecurity of domestic threat when the world stage again brought terror that required the use of a bomb shelter.

During the Cuban Missile Crisis two years later, my friends and I again experienced protective confinement in fallout shelters. These actions by adults who feared losing their children through the violence of nuclear destruction or sexual assault and murder conflated sexual and political violence in my seven–year-old mind. Time was compressed and the differences between personal traumas and political threat were erased; both became a single event.

Through a coincidence, the circumstances of my childhood unconsciously fused sexual and political violence into a single message of threat and terror. Novelties coupled by happenstance in 1960, unremitting threats of nuclear annihilation and sexual assault are, today, rendered as a single banal message. The fusion of sexual and political violence, no longer exceptional, is a staple of the entertainment industry that aggressively markets a culture of sexual terror, political intrigue, terrorism, and war. In this culture of sexual predation, contemporary news coverage of actual warfare evokes our private "war stories" of sexual threat, creating a public narrative of war that purposely fuses sexual and political violence. This nexus, once coincidental, then commonplace, now is calculated.

I recently presented a paper at a politics and mass communication conference in which I compared violent scenes from the film *Un Chien Andalou* with a battery, murder, and rape scene from the television series "Twin Peaks." I gave what I thought was a strong warning about the graphic violence and stopped the films during my presentation to make points about techniques and meaning. I gave an extra warning before the murder of Laura Palmer's look-alike cousin, Maddy, by her uncle (Laura's father, who had also raped and murdered his daughter). Although this scene aired during prime time and was watched by millions of fans, I was completely unprepared for the effect that watching this ferocious attack would have on my audience. I had worked with these texts to the point of numbness myself and had forgotten the sheer length of the scene with the bludgeoning, which lasted several minutes, and how the symbolic reinforcement of surrealist techniques are meant to plumb the viewers' psychic depths. I watched my audience cover their ears and eyes, then sit in stunned silence at the end of the taped example. I received two polite questions from men about the history of the surrealist movement during the discussion period and a flood of personal recollections from women who spoke to me privately at the end of the session. These events caused me to reconsider ever using such visuals again. Yet, when a colleague who uses very similar material gave a presentation in another situation without visual examples, she was peppered with comments, suggesting that she was being too hard on "Twin Peaks," had little appreciation for art, and, like every other feminist, was merely an ideologue raising complaints that inevitably resulted in authoritarian political correctness and censorship.

These experiences suggest to me that some materials do, in fact, speak for themselves. Yet, as a teacher, I also believe that learning is not a matter of "being right" in a confrontation that teaches through force and harm. In such presentations I would now describe, in as detailed a way as possible, the length of the example, the action that will be viewed, the type of sounds that will be heard, and the point the film clip makes in the context of the presentation. I will suggest that the audience need not view the example if my presentation has given them a logical and theoretical basis for accepting the point that this example illustrates. I will offer to make the example available for later viewing by anyone who would like to see it, if students decide later that they need this information.

Sut Jhally, an associate professor of communication at the University of Massachusetts at Amherst, and the creator of "Dreamworlds" (a video that examines the depiction of women on MTV), used this method of framing emotionally charged materials in terms of the students' viewing choice in his own classroom. In one segment of "Dreamworlds," Jhally juxtaposes scenes from the movie *The Accused* in which a woman is gang-raped on a pool table, with clips from MTV videos, until viewers are unable to determine where the rape ends and where MTV begins.[1] Jhally stops the video and takes a short break right before the rape scene. He recalls:

The first time I showed "Dreamworlds" to my class in its present form, I didn't give a strong enough warning. I said there's some stuff on here that people may not like, and it could be very disturbing, and they shouldn't stay if they don't want to. But I guess I wasn't clear enough that this was a voluntary activity. There was one woman who came to me afterwards, totally shaken, and said that she had lived through this, she did not need to be reminded of it. So I'm very careful now to really stress that this is a voluntary activity, that people know the extent of the images. The interesting thing is it depends on what you think the violent images are. Because the rape scene from *The Accused* is one thing, but all the other images, of course, are what is on the media. They're normal. And to the extent that you can actually make them problematic, then the video works to the extent that these videos which are seen as normal become extraordinary.[2]

MAKING THE CLASSROOM A SAFE ENVIRONMENT

Film represents popular culture's fusion of sexual and political domination. As a narrative text, however, film also provides an important instructional tool, helping us gain insight into political violence. Visual media's ability to convey powerful messages, combined with real-life issues of sexuality can make the topic of sexual violence a difficult one for classroom discussions. Using potent, and sometimes graphic, visual imagery to convey sensitive material in the classroom (any material that evokes strong emotional reactions, particularly about issues regarding sex, gender, violence, ethnicity or race) can trigger unforeseen emotional responses. Given the pervasiveness of the culture of sexual terror, many students and instructors come to class with personal narratives of sexual violence. Often an individual herself or himself fails to anticipate her or his response to film texts that touch such realities in the text of daily life. If popular visual representations of sexual and political violence do reduce our capacities as self-governing citizens, as this essay suggests, we must face this challenging teaching situation and increase our students' "visual literacy" and ability to analyze film texts. This difficult teaching situation can be mollified by eliminating the element of emotional and pedagogical surprise.

Clearly stated goals that provide a framework for viewing films can be key to the effective use of film in the classroom. Such goals could include:

1. To increase awareness and understanding of how society primes and reinforces sexual violence through film and TV.

2. To develop analytical skills for distinguishing between sexual violence and political violence.

3. To identify the political implications of sexual violence, sexism, racism, homophobia, and other oppressions.

4. To identify variables that affect a person's perceptions of violence, such as personal experience, gender, age, and race.

5. To increase awareness of how sexual terror can deny a person's ability to make choices and participate in a society based on liberal principles of freedom and self-government.

The syllabus, as a contract between teacher and student, is a good vehicle for describing each film in detail and for indicating specifically what kind of material will be presented and when. In addition to having clear instructions about the materials and ample notice, students need the option to learn the basic information from alternative materials. A level of control and choice concerning whether one will view a particular film or visual presentation creates a safe environment for handling tough issues. It also protects students from feeling as if they were a captive audience, forced to experience sexually explicit scenes, graphic violence, racism, sexism, or homophobia.

A safe classroom first allows students to make their own decisions about whether they will view a particular film or visual presentation. As a next step, students and instructor can establish specific guidelines for participating in class discussions and for reviewing these agreements periodically. Stopping the screening of a film during a class presentation, and even taking a short break, is a clear message to the students that a conscious, self-governing citizen can choose to leave the room during the viewing of a sensitive scene.

Materials for film discussions provide another opportunity to be clear about instructional goals. Discussion questions can be very useful in setting guidelines that focus on the purpose for viewing the films, beginning with questions that ask the students what they saw in the film and what connections they made between the film and politics. While some material may challenge students intellectually and provoke deep assessment of personal beliefs, any "uncomfortable learning" can unintentionally be experienced as emotionally manipulative.

Film violence "primes" or evokes memories and feelings of intimidation and terror surrounding a personal experience. What is true in the general culture is probably so in the classroom as well. Even violence that is not explicitly sexual may prime actual experiences of sexual violence or the lessons taught by the culture of sexual terror. Instructors who try to draw out the culturally constructed nexus of sexual and political violence in the classroom find themselves in a challenging teaching situation: We want our instruction to provide the basis for critical thinking about this nexus, not to find ourselves recreating the narrative of popular culture ourselves. How can this nexus be explored, but not replicated? Since it is highly probable that the personal experience of sexual violence will influence how someone interprets and understands violence portrayed in film, this may be one situation where it is appropriate to make a number of assumptions about your students. Unfortunately, it is fairly safe to assume that many of your students have personally experienced some form of sexual violence. Additional assumptions that may help alleviate unforeseen emotional reactions in a classroom setting are:

1. Assume that triggering emotional responses from personal experience greatly impedes a student's ability to respond to the film at an intellectual level.

2. Assume that most students have not received professional assistance in dealing with emotional issues surrounding their personal experiences of sexual violence, increasing the possibility that the classroom could become a therapeutic setting.

3. Assume that some students do not want to disclose their personal experiences in the classroom setting, while others will try to create a forum for themselves and use the classroom to work through these issues.

4. Assume that some students not only lack emotional maturity to deal with their peers' self-disclosure, they also lack knowledge about the social meaning of a personal experience, for example, rape or incest.

5. Assume that even if students have the self-awareness of a personal experience, they may not know how this affects their perceptions, nor have the intellectual leverage to grasp the broader implications to society.

At the very least, we can assume that it could be embarrassing, painful, or uncomfortable for students to be in a discussion about sexuality if they have no experience or, if they have had a negative one. Student's own assumptions toward each other are probably more important than the assumed or real attitudes of the teacher. While teachers may be quite capable of dealing sensitively with students' questions or statements, their peers may not be. It is also important to acknowledge that experiences of violence differ according to gender. Men are less often the object of sexual terror than women and, when they are, they, as objects, are often feminized, underscoring the gendered nature of sexual terror. It is no small task therefore, to create a safe forum for discussing these issues, for it involves nothing less than an attempt to sensitize the whole class to a number of variables that affect our understanding and perceptions of the nature of sexual and political violence.

A simple method to raise students' awareness of the range of experiences that may affect our perceptions is to collect personal narratives and reading materials about the kinds of stories that may make up a classroom community. My own particular experience of these issues is presented to tell the reader about the emotional impact of such an experience on my life. The reader, however, is not invited to get involved with my emotions, but rather to think about the theoretical and pedagogical meaning of one person's story. If it seems helpful, this could be an appropriate personal narrative for your use in planning classroom exercises.

Finally, it is important to identify appropriate forums for dealing clearly with the private and public aspects of sensitive issues. To underscore this point for the student, it is helpful to distribute a list of campus and community resources available to students who are dealing with specific problems such as rape, incest, or sexual assault. This is the time for us, as teachers, to remember that emotionally disturbing experiences in the classroom setting, or even unwanted discomfort, not only violates the students' rights for intellectual freedom, but can diminish their potential for intellectual enlightenment.

Developing critical thinking skills is essential for maintaining freedom of choice within a culture of violence. It is, therefore, imperative that we keep in mind that familiarity with a topic, unaccompanied by knowledge of a topic, not only produces unsophisticated thinking, it also prevents the development of empathy for another's experience.

MAKING THE CLASSROOM SAFE: AN EXERCISE

Reviewing basic listening skills can be indispensable in creating a safe learning environment for analyzing political violence through film. The following three-way conversation exercise is designed to develop the active listening skills necessary for exchanging ideas and opinions about sensitive materials and can be a good start.

Divide the class into three-person groups. Prepare these group assignments with the class roster, keeping in mind the students' personalities as well as their listening, leadership, and analytical skills as observed in at least five class sessions. Consider how age, gender, race, and class standing may interact in the groups.

For the exercise, choose a topic from your course that students have enough information about to have formed a point of view (i.e., data, logical connections, opinions that expose personal assumptions and logic to others). Each member of the three-person groups will take turns playing speaker, listener, and moderator. For the first moderator of a group, choose a student who has leadership abilities, including the ability to give directions in a corrective but non-judgmental way and the ability to encourage participation through her or his example.

Ask person "a" to tell person "b" about the issue (examples: my view on abortion, what I think is the gender issue in this movie, what I think of "just war" criteria). Ask B to listen and when A is finished, B is to repeat as closely as possible what A said. B should add nothing to make the explanation clearer or more palatable to A, nor should B leave out anything. A can then have a chance to clarify or explain further. C plays the role of disinterested judge. If C hears B embellish the story or lead A to a conclusion that is not true to A's intended meaning, C stops B and corrects the presentation. If C hears B repeat A's message in a true-to-the-story way and A changes her story, C stops A and says that while it's all right for A to change and amend her original position, A must tell B that B accurately attributed the correct position to A. In other words, B did get the message, and if A doesn't like it when it's played back, that's fine, but it's a different issue. Changing one's mind is different from saying I never had that position. The point of the assignment is to develop listening skills, to develop trust, to empower people to "own" their ideas, and to empower them to change their point of view rather than deny their point of view.

NOTES

1. Fred Pelk, "'Dreamworlds': How the Media Abuses Women," *On the Issues*, Winter 1991, 22.
2. Ibid, 40.

7

Why Did the Chicken Cross the Screen? Cognitive and Emotional Considerations in Using Film to Teach about the Manhattan Project and Hiroshima

David Pace

CAUTIONARY TALE #1: A SHORT MOVIE ABOUT A CHICKEN

In the 1950s, a sanitary official decided to use film to teach nonliterate members of a third-world society to get rid of standing water. Actors were shown slowly and deliberately draining pools and removing tins that might collect water. At the end of the first screening in the field, the audience was asked to comment on the film. The response of all the thirty-odd viewers was the same: they reported having seen a chicken. Only when they were pressed did they indicate that they had also noticed a man moving water.

The amazed filmmakers carefully reexamined the film and found that a chicken did, indeed, cross the frame for about a second. But for the audience, which did not share either the concerns or the conventions of the filmmakers, the chicken was the star of the show.[1]

CAUTIONARY TALE #2: A SLIGHTLY LONGER MOVIE ABOUT A BOMB

Professor Smedlap turned off the lights, and the class watched a film about the destruction of Hiroshima. As he looked at the horrifying images of destruction, the instructor felt just a little smug. "This will make them think," he said to himself.

Smedlap would not have been so sure of himself had he observed the behavior of his students in the period immediately after class. Most of them exited as quickly as possible and immediately looked for distractions to ex-punge the images of nuclear destruction from their minds. But the small group of students who did continue to talk about the film would have given their instructor little to be happy about. One student claimed to have been fascinated by the gory images and tried to "gross out" the others by making jokes about the scenes they had just witnessed. Another student said noth-ing, but these comments pushed her near the edge. Unresolved issues with her parents, a betrayal by a friend, a course on the Holocaust, this film, and her classmate's outrageous behavior had all blurred together to produce a sense that life was probably not worth living. Nearby another group of stu-dents were arguing about the issues raised in the film. One said that the Japa-nese deserved it all because they bombed Pearl Harbor. Another insisted that the American leaders must have been monsters to use the weapon, and a third argued that war is about killing and that once it has started the only thing to do is kill enough people to make it end fast. All the students were disturbed, but none seemed to be doing very much critical thinking.

These stories, the first real and the second fictitious, are worth remember-ing when using film to teach about violence. Film is an extraordinarily pow-erful teaching tool. It can cause students to confront material on the level of the concrete, where fundamental breakthroughs in understanding are most likely to occur. And it has enormous affective power. Film can help students understand why the material studied in class is important.

But the very concreteness of film makes it open to the imposition of many meanings. Editing techniques and shared conventions of viewing a film will generally produce a loose consensus about the basic narrative of most films. Yet, while we may not face in the classroom the kind of total misunderstand-ing our hygienists encountered in the bush, there are always a great variety of possible meanings that can be found in any film.

To a certain extent this is no problem. Most of us would agree that it is not the role of an instructor to impose a particular worldview on a student. And differences of interpretation among members of a class can be an enormous resource for discussion. At a certain point, however, the instructor may find him or herself in the position of the public health officials cited above. The instructor wants the class to think seriously about drinking water, but the students are obsessed with the chicken. The concerns and suppositions that they have brought into the class have completely overpowered learning.

This problem is particularly serious when dealing with issues concerning violence, whether it be overt or structural. Violence is a matter of over-whelming concern to virtually every human being on the planet. From childhood, we have each developed certain protective mechanisms to deal with it. We have learned to use it, threaten it, deflect it, and resist it. These patterns are so essential to our survival that, once they have been evoked, the experience of viewing a film may be entirely structured around them.

The tendency of issues of violence to distort learning processes is nowhere more visible than in the study of the first use of nuclear weapons. The inability of the Smithsonian to mount a retrospective exhibit for the fiftieth anniversary of the destruction of Hiroshima and Nagasaki serves as a clear reminder that teaching about the development and initial use of the atomic bomb may easily be drowned out by an emotional clamor. Not only has the beginning of the "atomic age" become intertwined with questions of national honor, but two generations of Americans, who have grown up under the threat of nuclear annihilation, have projected their hopes and fears back upon this period. While the intensity of this fear may lessen, as more and more students come to consciousness after the end of the Cold War, the mushroom cloud remains both a collective and an individual symbol of a vast array of terrors. Simply showing film footage of the horrors of Hiroshima and Nagasaki can easily activate these fears without generating serious thought.

Moreover, after a half century of repetition, most of the standard responses to the use of the bomb have dug such deep ruts in the collective consciousness that once students have fallen into a particular position, it is often very difficult for them to consider other possibilities. A film may simply trigger a particular dogma about the decision to use the weapon without generating serious consideration of the deeper historical and moral issues involved in that choice.

Thus, the responses of Smedlap's students to the scenes of nuclear devastation should be no surprise. The emotional power of these images was so great that many students sought to avoid thinking about them at all. A few used gross humor to dispel the threat and to create the illusion that they were unaffected by it. Some identified with the victims so much that their own psychological baggage became indistinguishable from their consideration of the event itself. Students who entered the course convinced that the use of the bomb was immoral generally had that position reinforced without necessarily gaining any better understanding of the historical context or the nature of the decision-making process. Those who started with the opposite position generally maintained their beliefs, although for many of them the effort to maintain these positions in the face of powerful scenes of human suffering reinforced their belief that "realists" had to remain unaffected by such emotional or moral concerns.

At the core of Professor Smedlap's problem lies a dilemma that anyone seeking to use film as an effective teaching tool must face. The very quality that makes film most useful in the classroom—its power to make students identify emotionally with people in a different situation—can prevent students from thinking critically about what they have seen. Playwright Bertolt Brecht faced a similar problem when he set out to use drama as a means of educating the public about social and political conditions. Since the time of Aristotle, emotional identification with the action on the stage had been seen as core of the experience of theater. But Brecht feared that this very identification would prevent his audience from rationally considering the material he presented on the stage. Therefore, he created a new "epic theater," which kept the audience at a distance from the action so that it could think clearly about what was being presented.

Many of the techniques through which Brecht sought to achieve this "alienation effect" are not available to the classroom instructor using film. We cannot, for example, make the characters on the screen act in an erratic manner in order to minimize identification. But we can learn from his efforts to contextualize actions by means of interruptions, explicit commentary on plot developments, and juxtaposition of contradictory interpretations. For example, the emotional trance produced by a film can be interrupted by stopping periodically to discuss the implications of what is begin shown and the manner in which the film structures its viewers' responses. Different films can be juxtaposed to give students a space from which to make judgments, and excerpts of film can be viewed out of context. Finally all films can be preceded and followed by lectures and readings containing contextual material designed to help students maintain a certain distance from what they are being shown.

BEYOND BRECHT

Taken to its extreme, the Brechtian project would eliminate the very power that makes film an attractive teaching tool in the first place. If it were possible entirely to eliminate any emotional identification with a film, there would rarely be a reason to spend class time showing it. Readings, lectures, and discussions are generally better vehicles for the transmission of information or the discussion of ideas. Moreover, if students are not allowed deep emotions in the classroom, they will be denied the opportunity to learn how to think clearly about issues that evoke passionate emotions.

Nonetheless, it is worth considering a middle path that creates a rhythm of emotional identification and rational distancing. Such a mixed strategy is precisely what was lacking in Smedlap's class. He assumed that just showing the film was enough. There was no framing process before the showing and no debriefing afterwards. Any processing of the film took place in a totally haphazard manner in the hallway after class. Nothing prevented emotions and ideas from running together and becoming confused.

USING FILM: AN ALTERNATIVE APPROACH

How might Smedlap have used the film differently? First, he might have been careful to assure that the students had all the information they needed in order to think critically about the issues raised in the film. In the case of the film about Hiroshima, he might have assigned readings or given lectures describing the decision-making process that led up the bombing, the general climate of opinion that surrounded it, and the discussions about how it should be used.

Secondly, he might have structured the experience of viewing the film in such a way that there was more room for rational analysis. He might, for example, have posed a series of questions in advance, which would have aided students in thinking about the event. If the impact of the film appeared to be so great that it was completely overwhelming cognitive processes, he might have fallen back on Brechtian strategies and interrupted the showing from time to time to raise questions that would make it more likely that students would think and feel at the same time.

Next, he might have provided students with models for feeling and thinking about such horrible events. Before and after the film, he could discuss the difficulties involved in combining these two functions and the importance of trying to do so. He, himself, could demonstrate both feeling and thinking about the horror, so that the students could begin to discriminate between the two.

All of this could be brought together in a debriefing session at the end of the film in which first affective responses and then intellectual analyses were given prominence. The class could be broken up into small groups in which each student, in turn, was asked to share his or her emotional response to what had been seen. The groups could report back on what was said and the legitimacy of these feelings could be honored. Then there could be an explicit transition to processing the film in terms of the initial questions.

The instructor showing films with powerful emotional impact is always playing a complex balancing act. If the students seem to be so overwhelmed by emotions that they cannot think clearly, then it is time for an intervention. On the other hand, if the students seem to be avoiding all explicit emotional contact with the issues, it may be wise to try to encourage more identification. Here the process is the reverse of that of Brecht. One should focus on concrete scenes, rather than on abstractions, and on personal responses, rather than statements about the world. This emotional processing may be very important because if the students avoid explicitly confronting their feelings, these emotions may contaminate any attempt to think about the implications of these events.

Clear modeling of both thinking and feeling about violence and a structural separation of the two processes can help those students who are inclined to incorporate a film into their preexisting emotional patterns to learn to think more clearly about these issues. But what about the other students mentioned above—the one who focused entirely on Pearl Harbor, the second who thought the Americans were all monsters, and the third who argued that once war began all moral issues involving the use of violence disappeared? As in the case of the students who were emersed in emotional issues, it is likely that each of these students is just replaying a schema, which he or she has applied to many other situations in the past. But this time the schemes may have more to do with cognitive structures and protocols for posing moral questions than with emotional patterns.

It is important to note that each of these students has something very important to say. The first recognizes that the destruction of Hiroshima is not an isolated event, but rather is linked to broader events in the war. The second understands that this decision involved some basic moral issues and that the motivations of American leaders must be examined. The third student has recognized that this decision cannot be fully understood outside the context of a wartime mentality. Yet, each student is locked in a rather simplistic universe. How are we to assist students in gaining more complex ways of dealing with such questions.

This first step is to recognize that the limitations of each of these students may be related to the development of his or her cognitive faculties. As William Perry has suggested in his classic study *Forms of Intellectual and Ethical Development in the College Years*,[2] many of our students may not yet have mastered the basic mental operations needed to perform the seemingly simple tasks that we expect of them. Perry explained his ideas through a parallel with developmental processes in children described by Jean Piaget. Piaget observed that, before a certain age, infants seemed unable to recognize that two sides of an object were part of the same whole. They were unable to understand that a thing could look different from different perspectives. Perry argued that similar limitations are present among many college students trying to grapple with questions of value. The ability to understand that a complex moral issue may not look the same from different perspectives is not, he insisted, automatically present in all students. It is a complex skill that develops over time and through a series of definite stages.

While Perry's stages of cognitive development are unnecessarily rigid, his general model can still provide relevant insights into the ways in which students process film in the classroom. According to Perry, most students began by thinking about moral questions in terms of absolute authority. All actions are established as either moral or immoral on some external and absolute scale. Like infants who do not understand that a single object has many sides, they assume that there is only one real way of viewing any situation, and the notion that the values and life experiences of an individual inevitably shape his or her perception of an issue is beyond their comprehension.

For such students, the demands of an instructor to become involved in critical thinking are meaningless. Faced with a situation, they are convinced that their task is to apply a fixed standard and to determine which "answer" is the correct one. If they are asked to compare and contrast two points of view, they often become confused and feed back a recitation of facts, rather than an evaluation of the merits of conflicting interpretations. And such students will often fail to understand why and how evidence is used to make a particular position more credible than another.

Two of the students described above appear to fall, at least in part, into this category. The first framed the issues in terms of one moral commandment: all Japanese were guilty because their government started the war. The other came to the opposite conclusion by comparing the images in the film to moral commandments, such as "Thou shalt not kill."

In itself, there is nothing necessarily wrong about either position. But the processes by which such absolute positions are often arrived at may not be conducive to the kind of critical thinking that the instructor had hoped to spark. It is quite likely that neither student had mastered the ability to balance the relative merits of different interpretations of the events. They probably could not explore the possibility that different moral imperatives might be in conflict in this situation, nor could they examine the historical context in which these decisions were generated.

The final student, who believed that everything was justified in wartime, probably represents a "higher" level on Perry's scale. Here is a student, who can easily entertain the possibility of different perspectives on an issue, but she lacks any criteria for determining the relative validity of rival propositions. In this situation, she has no basis for differentiating between an individual who is willing to defend his or her country with limited means from the women who, after the destruction of Hiroshima, advocated blasting "the four Jap islands into oblivion" before the population "could breed more of the same kind of soldiers to make us trouble in the future."[3] This student is still not able to make the kind of careful evaluation of conflicting claims expected in most classrooms, and she continues to live in a world in which "that's your opinion" is the ultimate refutation.

If we accept Perry's assertion that at least some of the difficulties students have in dealing with complex moral questions has to do with their cognitive organization, how are we to help them gain access to more complex ways of approaching questions? We can, of course, avoid the entire question by saying that it is not the job of the instructor to change the basic ways students process issues morally. But such a position is only consistent if students can operate effectively in the course on the basis of dualistic mental organization. None of the three students considered above is in a position to weigh alternatives, to compare and contrast attitudes, or to consider issues from multiple perspectives, and these operations may be necessary for success in the course.

Thus, while we have no moral right to force students to accept certain approach to moral reasoning, we do have an obligation to give them the opportunity to add new methods of mental processing to their existing repertoire. This, however, can be quite difficult. If Perry is correct, we are dealing here, not with a simple idea that can be debated, but rather with a fundamental means of organizing reality. Everything that a student is told will be understood within the context of his or her existing mental structures.

Using film is no automatic solution to this problem. It can, in fact, reinforce simplistic procedures of moral reasoning. Most Hollywood films and many documentaries tend to be framed in terms of a single objective standard of moral judgment and leave little room for ambiguity or differing perspectives. And those films that seek to undercut common views of society can serve to reinforce a student in Perry's "relativist" stage that no opinion is more valuable than any other.

Yet, film can provide a means of breaking through students' existing mental structures and of providing them with the opportunity to develop more complex strategies. Because the words of the instructor will almost always be interpreted in terms of existing cognitive structures, it is important to shift learning to a more concrete and immediate level of learning. By its very nature, film is concrete, and it is at this level, not at that of abstraction, that basic cognitive changes are most apt to occur.

Thus, film can be particularly useful in making different perspectives real for a student. In the case of teaching about the Manhattan Project and Hiroshima, an instructor could show relevant scenes from two or more films that present the relevant issues from very different perspectives or from a single film that dramatized the intellectual and moral conflicts among those involved in the development of the first nuclear weapons.

A passive viewing of one or many scenes, however, is not apt to make students break through to more complex ways of dealing with such questions. This kind of cognitive change will generally emerge only after they themselves have been encouraged to view the use of the bomb from more than one perspective. Therefore, the viewing of the film should be accompanied by a carefully structured pedagogical experience, which will automatically create a situation in which this shift of perspectives is natural.

The simplest way to embody multiple perspectives in the classroom would be a straightforward debate of the issues. Yet, even if the debate is made more complex by having students change positions in midstream, there remains a strong possibility that the interaction will cause them to harden their positions, rather than becoming open to other possibilities. An alternative would be to follow the showing of a particular scene with a structured exercise in which groups of students are asked to play the roles of types of individuals they have just seen on the screen. In a treatment of the Manhattan Project, for example, different groups might be assigned the roles of a military officer, a civilian scientist, or a government official. Then, the groups would be asked to recreate the conflicts that ensued over the development and the use of the atomic bomb. Before the interactions begin, each group could be asked to consider the kinds of factors that might affect its position (professional training, personal interests, life experiences, concerns about recent history, etc.).

Such a process would automatically give students a kind of "binocular" vision of the events, as they would simultaneously see the relevant issues from their own perspective and from that of the character they are role-playing. At the end of the interaction, a debriefing session would allow students the opportunity to discuss the merits and weaknesses of each position as well as the kinds of historical conditions that helped shaped each point of view.

This kind of pedagogical structure places students who are searching for absolutes in a paradoxical position. The exercise makes them imagine how things might appear differently to different individuals. To take part in the exercise, they must view events as their character would, while remaining aware of their own interpretation of the situation. This multiperspectival experience is in implicit tension with their own notion that there is only one "real" perspective on events.

There is no assurance that such an experience will automatically give a student more cognitive tools for dealing with moral questions. And, in fact, in many cases it should not. For many students, moral absolutism is part of a personal ecology which it would be inappropriate to disturb. But for other students, who are ready for such an experience, the concrete perspectives embodied in a film can provide a means of achieving more complex strategies for dealing with such questions.

There remain, however, those students who are in the great swamp of relativism. The very exercise that provides the other students with an opportunity to expand their cognitive strategies can serve to reinforce the cognitive patterns of these students. The experience of different moral positions within a film, followed by a role-playing exercise using those characters, can make them more willing than ever to assume that all opinions are equal and that there is no basis for discrimination.

For these students, it is necessary to move beyond the experience of multiple perspectives to that of evaluating the strength of different arguments. In the case described above, it might be wise to add an exercise after the role-playing in which students present evidence that each character might advance in support of his or her position. The evidence of different characters could then be compared and contrasted in a discussion, which would provide an implicit model of how to construct criteria of judgment.

In all of these pedagogical strategies, the focus has been upon the student's processing of film, not the film itself. It is, however, also important to choose films carefully so as to be certain that they will provide the basis for the kinds of critical thinking the instructor is seeking to encourage. In the case of the decision to use an atomic bomb against Hiroshima and Nagasaki there is an abundance of materials to choose from.

FILMS ABOUT THE ISSUES

Among the many documentaries that deal with these issues three are particularly useful: "Dawn," the first video in the series *War and Peace in the Nuclear Age*, *Day after Trinity*, and *Atomic Cafe*.[4]

"Dawn"

This episode from *War and Peace in the Nuclear Age* provides a good overview of the development of the atomic bomb, and it might be effectively used to reinforce ideas in the reading. While any presentation of nuclear issues must have a point of view, this video attempts to present a consensus view of the Manhattan Project and the decision to use the new weapon—to the extent that a consensus exists among professional historians. It will probably be more useful on an intellectual than on an affective plane.

The Day after Trinity

The Day after Trinity, by contrast, is a perfect film for introducing students to the moral dilemmas raised by the atomic bomb. Focusing largely on the career of Robert Oppenheimer, it very effectively presents the shifting motivations for developing the weapon. Perhaps the most important sections of the documentary are the interviews with participants in the Manhattan Project, who struggle on camera to examine the morality of their own involvement and that of their fellow scientists.

Atomic Cafe

While most of *Atomic Cafe* is devoted to the Cold War and the development of a nuclear culture in the 1950s, the first section of the documentary can be very useful in providing students with powerful images. Scenes of the damage at Hiroshima and Nagasaki, of the victims of the explosions, of President Truman's gleeful announcement of the use of the bomb, of press conferences with the pilots who carried the weapons to their targets, and of the creation of a surreal propaganda film at Bikini atoll—all of this can make concrete and meaningful the beginning of the nuclear era.

The Beginning or the End

Hollywood has attempted on three occasions to portray the events leading up to the destruction of Hiroshima and Nagasaki. While none of these efforts have been great cinematic triumphs, each of them contains scenes that can be highly useful in teaching about this period. The first of these films, *The Beginning or the End* (1947),[5] used all the conventions of wartime propaganda films to portray the Manhattan Project as a totally selfless and harmonious burst of cooperation in the service of a goal that needed no justification. Juxtaposed to a description of the same events in a serious work of history such as Martin Sherwin's *A World Destroyed*,[6] *The Beginning or the End* can open students' eyes to the way in which the telling of a story can radically affect its moral significance. The presentation of military officers, political leaders, scientists, and industrialists in the film can be used as the basis for a role-playing exercise, such as the one mentioned above, and the moral justifications for American policy provided in the film can serve as a basis for discussion.

Enola Gay

The Beginning or the End was a classic Hollywood potboiler, and the next feature film on the making of the bomb, *Enola Gay* (1980),[7] was not much better. In 150 agonizingly slow minutes, the film presents events from the perspective of the bomber crews who were preparing to drop the bomb.

With little concern for historical accuracy, the fliers are transformed into Hollywood men-of-action whose humorous interactions and personal problems are obviously supposed to recreate the spirit of World War II films. There is little for students to learn from *Enola Gay* about the real preparations for dropping the bomb, but, like *The Beginning or the End*, it can be used to present a particular set of justifications for the use of the bomb, and it can help students become more aware of how films can shape our perceptions of events. One might, for example, ask students to discuss the fact that in the closing minutes of the film the only people shown in the streets of Hiroshima were soldiers drilling.

Fat Man and Little Boy

The most recent film about the Manhattan Project, *Fat Man and Little Boy* (1989),[8] is a much more serious attempt to deal with these issues. While it also amplifies events to create drama, it relies on a higher level of acting and a more serious script than do its predecessors. Moreover, while *Fat Man and Little Boy* was created from at least as strong an ideological position as its predecessors, it presents a systematic critique of the decisions taken in 1945 and, thus, provides a useful contrast to the other films. While the presentation of the moral dilemmas of the atomic scientists are captured more effectively in the interviews in *The Day after Trinity*, this film raises questions about the nature of the personal and institutional factors that shaped nuclear policy and, thus, could make an important contribution to class discussion.

It would almost certainly be a bad idea to show of any of these plodding feature films in its entirety to a class, and even the documentaries will generally be more effective if they are presented in sections over several class periods interspersed with background lectures and/or discussions. Fortunately, the sections of the *The Beginning or the End* that were directly related to the development of the atomic bomb have been separated from the melodrama that surrounded them in the original film, and this 30-minute version is available for classroom use.[9] *Enola Gay* and *Fat Man and Little Boy* are both available on video, which makes it easier to show carefully selected excerpts to a class. As these films contain dramatizations of the same events, it would be possible to produce a *"Rashomon"* effect by creating a collage of such scenes. By following these scenes from the feature films with excerpts from the documentaries, it would also be possible to juxtapose Hollywood images of the scientists of the Manhattan Project or the pilots who carried the atomic bomb with their real-life counterparts.

Thus, there is an abundant supply of relevant and readily available material for anyone wishing to use film to teach about Hiroshima and the Manhattan Project. Yet, it must be stressed once again that the success of such learning experiences depends upon making the film a part of a larger pedagogical strategy. We cannot assume that showing a film, in itself, will necessarily lead students to think more effectively about issues of violence. We must be sure that the affective responses to the film are in balance with thinking about these issues. And we must consider the kinds of cognitive structures the students bring to the experience and create experiences that offer them the possibility of adding new processes to their repertoire. Only after we have placed the films within the context of such a pedagogical strategy can we begin to have reasonable expectations that our students will see something besides the "chicken."

NOTES

1. John Wilson, "Film Literacy in Africa," *Canadian Communications* 1, no. 4 (Summer 1961), 7–14. Quoted in Marshall McLuhan, *The Gutenberg Galaxy; The Making of Typographic Man* (Toronto: University of Toronto Press, 1962), 36–38.

2. William G. Perry, *Forms of Intellectual and Ethical Development in the College Years* (New York: Holt, Rinehart, and Winston, Inc., 1970).

3. Lawrence S. Wittner, *Rebels against War; The American Peace Movement, 1933–1983* (Philadelphia: Temple University Press, 1984), 129.

4. *War and Peace in the Nuclear Age, Part I*, "Dawn" (War and Peace in the Nuclear Age series); Annenberg/CPB Project, 1988, *Day After Trinity* (Pyramid Films, 1981); *Atomic Café* (Archives Project, 1982).

5. *The Beginning or the End* (MGM, 1946).

6. Martin J. Sherwin, *A World Destroyed: The Atomic Bomb and the Grand Alliance* (New York: Vintage Books, 1977).

7. *Enola Gay* (Los Angeles: Prism Entertainment, 1980).

8. *Fat Man and Little Boy* (Hollywood, CA: Paramount, 1989).

9. This abbreviated version of *The Beginning or the End* is available through the audiovisual departments of Indiana University and the University of Wisconsin.

Part III

Resources

8

Sample Study and Discussion Guides

John P. Lovell with contributions from William Meyer, Jean Robinson, Barbara Allen and Gloria Gibson

COMING TO TERMS WITH VIOLENCE AND PEACE

Overview

The term "violence" typically evokes in us images of acts in our domestic and international milieus that we especially deplore—armed gangs roaming the streets, child abuse, murder, rape, pillage, war. In contrast, the notion of a "peaceful society" or, better yet, a "peaceful world" evokes images of highly desirable environments.

But what do we mean by terms such as "violence" and "peace?" The purpose of this document is to provoke thought about some of the terms and ideas most germane to the films and to raise some issues that you might wish to discuss.

Violence

Let us begin by the term "violence." Is it appropriate to restrict the meaning of "violence" to direct physical assaults such as those alluded to above? Many scholars and social activists would answer emphatically "No!" for reasons that will be apparent in the films. There is physical violence in the film—but also emotional violence and assaults on human dignity.

It is probably no coincidence that many of the important ideas that contribute to an understanding of the multiple dimensions of violence in the human experience have been initiated by individuals especially concerned with Third World problems and perspectives. Examples of such ideas that are especially pertinent to the films that will be shown are the following:

When severe impediments to the realization of one's human potential are imposed, one may regard the thwarting of human potential as an act of violence. This act may be done by one actor or actors to another actor or actors, in which case what is occurring is oppression (Freire, 548). On the other hand, when the thwarting of human potential is the result of the social structure rather than of direct exploitation or oppression by others, this is a situation of structural violence. As Galtung observes, "If people are starving when this is objectively avoidable, then violence is committed, regardless of whether there is a clear subject action-object relation, as during a siege yesterday or no such clear relation, as in the way world economic relations are organized today (171)".

Films raise interesting and important questions about the relationships between oppressed and oppressor, as well as about relationships among the oppressed. Concerning the latter, Freire writes (based on his fieldwork in northeast Brazil):

The peasant is a dependent. He can't say what he wants. Before he discovers his dependence, he suffers. He lets off steam at home, where he shouts at his children, beats them, and despairs. He complains about his wife and thinks everything is dreadful. He doesn't let off steam with the boss because he thinks his boss is a superior being. Lots of times, the peasant gives vent to his sorrows by drinking. (155)

The hazards of ethnocentrism may only confound the difficulty in term of policy options. As a frame of reference, Berger postulates a situation in which an anthropologist, anxious to avoid passing judgment on the cannibalistic society he is studying (thereby exhibiting ethnocentrism), is asked to help the leadership of the society to formulate a development plan for the society. "Is the anthropologist meekly to assent" to the expressed desire of the leadership that the plan incorporate cannibalism, Berger asks. He notes that the example is not that extreme:

The Third World today is blessed with a number of development strategies that calmly include (implicitly or explicitly) the sacrifice of large numbers of human beings, be it by direct violence or by policies that deliberately refrain from alleviating suffering. Criticism of these strategies are routinely turned back by negative references to Western "ethnocentrism."(133)

The special susceptibility of women to violence (both physical and structural) is depicted in various ways in the films. Discussion groups might want to consider the following argument from a 1990 article by Charlotte Brunch:

Violence against women is not random—the risk factor is being female. Sex discrimination kills females from infancy when, according to the World Health Organization, more girls die of malnutrition, to adulthood where domestic battery is the leading cause of injury to women worldwide. Yet, the violence of sexism is rarely considered a political issue because it is relegated to the realm of the private, often even sanctioned by law, and dismissed as humorous by many. . .

Violence causes physical pain and mental disabilities threatening death through-out the female life cycle, from the fetus aborted because it is a girl to the widow abandoned because she is no longer considered useful. . .

Daily violence against women in the home, on the streets, and in the media is a major underpinning to acceptance of militarism as well as a direct contradiction to hopes for a peaceful world.

Peace

How shall we think about "peace?" On the one hand, many peace activists and scholars argue that is imperative to go beyond merely equating peace with the absence of war (organized physical violence). Rather, we should aspire to peace with justice—not merely "negative peace" but "positive peace." As a recent peace studies textbook explains:

Peace can and must include not only the absence of war but also the establishment of positive life-affirming and life-enhancing values and structures. . . . Positive peace. . . refers to a condition of society in which exploitation is minimized or eliminated altogether, and in which there is neither overt violence nor the more subtle phenomenon of structural violence. (Barash, 5,8)

On the other hand, it is important to recognize that not even all peace activists and peace researchers agree with the broad conceptualization of peace. Consider, for example, the concerns expressed in a recent commentary on new approaches in peace research:

It is not, I believe, helpful in work for peace to dilute the concept of violence by stretching it to include other evils which, as in the cases of "oppression" or "starvation," have their own names. Something precious is lost when the word "violence" is blurred. The real horror of war—which is not simply the dying, but the deliberate organization for killing, for engaging in mass, indiscriminate slaughter—is vitiated. . . . For many people thinking in this perspective [with "peace" expanded to include the elimination of "structural violence"], it is not until this point that international peace even becomes desirable. (Pickus, 231)

REFERENCES

Barash, David P. 1991. *Introduction to Peace Studies*. Belmont, CA: Wadsworth.

Berger, Peter. 1976. "'Consciousness Raising' and the Vicissitudes of Policy." In *Pyramids of Sacrifice*, edited by Peter Berger. New York: Anchor Books, chap. 4.

Bunch, Charlotte. 1990. "The Politics of Violence." *On the Issues*, Choices Women's Medical Center, Forest Hills, NY, Fall, 25.

Freire, Paulo. 1988. "Pedagogy of the Oppressed." In *Political Economy of Development and Underdevelopment*, 4th ed., edited by Charles Wilbur. New York: Random House, chap. 28.

Galtung, Johan. 1969. "Violence, Peace, and Peace Research." *Journal of Peace Research* 6:3, 167–191.

Pickus, Robert. 1991. "New Approaches." In *Approaches to Peace: An Intellectual Map*, edited by W. Scott Thompson and Kenneth M. Jensen. Washington, DC: U.S. Institute of Peace.

SAMPLE QUESTIONS FOR FILM WORKSHOP ON VIOLENCE AND STRUCTURAL VIOLENCE

1. What is "violence"?

2. What specifically is the violence in each of the films? Is the violence the same in each film?

3. Does structural violence justify physical violence? Compare and contrast the films' implicit responses to this question.

4. What do you consider to be the fundamental causes of structural violence?

5. How would you define the "good" life? What are the essential elements of such a life? What institutions are necessary to achieve that life?

6. Would you say that structural violence could be eliminated by providing people with greater material wealth (money, housing, etc.)? If so, who should make these sorts of allocative decisions?

SAMPLE QUESTIONS FOR FILM WORKSHOP ON "THE GOOD LIFE"

1. What society currently in existence comes closest to representing your ideal society? What are the reasons for your choice? How can we encourage "less-than-ideal" societies to change without causing more harm than good? Or is it none of our business?

2. What obligations do we have to respect a culture that deprives some of its members of what we in our own society consider basic human freedoms/rights/respect?

3. What responsibilities do we have to those affected by the changes we impose/urge?

4. Do we have any obligations to share what we have with others? What principles can we call on to guide us? Must we share if we disapprove of the lifestyle or of choices made by those who lay claim to what we have?

5. Some have said we need to pay less attention to a Bill of Rights than a Bill of Responsibilities. Is the idea of a Bill of Responsibilities appealing to you? If so, what would you include in it? How would you enforce it?

6. In the films that involve law, would you say that law makes the protagonists' situations better or worse, or both? In the other films, can you envision a role for law or government that would improve the protagonists' lives?

7. Is any/some of the structural violence within this society the result of too much freedom?

8. How can we make "doing good" more attractive than "doing well?" Is it appropriate even to try?

SAMPLE QUESTIONS FROM WILLIAM MEYER

Do the Right Thing

1. What are the sources that inhibit blacks in the neighborhood from owning their own businesses?

2. Is it wrong for Sal not to include pictures of African Americans on the wall of his Italian pizzeria? Why or why not? Does it matter that his customers are almost exclusively African Americans? Is it appropriate for him to celebrate his Italian American identity (the pictures on the wall are all of famous Italian Americans) in his place of business? What is this dispute about?—economic power, race, cultural pride and identity, values? What would bring about peace in this situation?—to empower African Americans to own their own restaurants with their own sets of pictures on the wall; to persuade Sal to celebrate the identities of his customers as well as his own ethnic identity; to persuade him to take down the pictures altogether; to persuade the African-American customer not to be offended by the pictures on the wall?

3. What is the underlying source of conflict between Sal and Radio Raheem? Was it an unfortunate ventilation of anger due to a lack of social justice? Or was it due to a conflict between different cultural values—due to different conceptions of what makes life good and/or civil? Is Radio Raheem's high-volume music box, at root, a form of protest against economic inequality and social injustice, or is it more reflective of some deeper cultural conception of the good life? Would Radio Raheem gladly turn down his high-volume music if social conditions and opportunities for African Americans were significantly improved, or is this more than a form of protest? How would liberals respond to this situation?—would they tell Radio Raheem that he can only play his loud music within the confines of his private living space? How would communitarians re-

spond? Would they say that Radio Raheem's music is meant to be communal and, thus, shared publicly with others in the community? But what does one do when there are different communities with their different conceptions of the good life in the same neighborhood?

The Grapes of Wrath

1. What are the underlying forms of violence and the underlying conceptions of peace and the good life?

2. What are the social, cultural, natural, and/or economic forces that prevent the Oklahoma families from maintaining their homes and way of life?

3. What are the contrasting images of capitalism versus socialism?

4. How would liberals and communitarians each interpret this film?

A Raisin in the Sun

1. How does one reconcile the conflicts between the family members and their differing conceptions of how to spend the money, that is, their differing conceptions of happiness and the good life?

2. How should they decide what to spend the money on? How would liberals and communitarians approach this issue?

Theme Found in All Three Films: Homogeneity vs Plurality

1. Is it always morally wrong to want to maintain the status quo/homogeneity of a community and, thus, to discourage new arrivals who are different? Why or why not? Was it morally wrong for the Californians not to want the "Okies" to move in (Grapes of Wrath)? Was it wrong for the group of young blacks to tell the young white man that he should go back to Boston (Do the Right Thing)? Was it wrong for the white homeowners to seek to pay the black family not to move into their neighborhood (A Raisin in the Sun)?

2. If there is moral wrong in all three cases, what are the reasons or bases for this conclusion? Might one argue that life, by nature, is dynamic and evolving and, therefore, that one ought always to embrace change rather than resist it?; that one has a moral obligation to seek maximal creativity/unity in the midst of diversity? But is change always creative rather than destructive? How can one judge whether change will be for the better or for the worse? As a precautionary measure, can residents of a community accept new arrivals but insist that they conform to the norms and values of the community? Or would this be wrong precisely because it embraces the status quo rather than dynamism?

3. Is a pluralistic community morally or normatively better than distinct ethnic communities or neighborhoods? Why? Are integrated communities or ethnically distinct ones more likely to foster peace and tolerance?

4. Is it ever morally permissible to resist the inclusion of outsiders into a neighborhood or community? What are the bases for this judgment? Are there any legitimate grounds for discouraging the inclusion of outsiders into a community? Is there a moral distinction between the act of discouraging outsiders from coming in and the act of encouraging those already there to leave?

SAMPLE QUESTIONS FROM JEAN ROBINSON

The most important effect of watching these films is to get students to consider new ways to answer the old questions:

Men and Women

1. What are the male protagonists doing? Why are they doing this?
2. What are the female protagonists doing? Why are they doing this?
3. Can you imagine a man acting the way the woman character acts? Why/why not?
4. How would this film be different if women were in positions of domination and men were subordinate?
5. What would it mean if men were primarily viewed as sex objects?

Power

1. Under what conditions do women have control?
2. Under what conditions do men have power?
3. What does the film tell us about why these changes occur and their effects?

Gender and Value

1. Does this film have a message about violence?
2. Are women "naturally" less violent than men?
3. Is this an innate characteristic? What makes characteristics innate or natural?

Students must be given the opportunity to think through the characters' actions and to place them in the context of the social setting of the film. They might than be asked to play around with the changes in setting, sex, power arrangements, and the like. Such an exercise will demonstrate the ways in which configurations of power are constructed.

SAMPLE QUESTIONS FROM BARBARA ALLEN

Surrealism

1. Compare and contrast the use of surrealist technique in *Un Chien Andalou* and "Twin Peaks." Discuss the effect on the viewer expected in each case.

2. What is "political" about this technique? Do we need to know the author's intention or does the technique "speak for itself?"

Cape Fear

1. Compare the major themes for the two versions of *Cape Fear*. How is stalking handled in each case? How should the law handle this issue? What is the role of law compared to the rule of patriarchy in each film?

2. Compare and contrast the culpability and innocence of each main character in the two versions of *Cape Fear*. Consider especially the authors' attitudes toward Danielle's role in the saga.

3. What issues besides gender are raised in the two versions of *Cape Fear*? What can you say about the issues of race and social class, for example?

Wertmueller

1. Consider the nexus of political and sexual violence or rule by force presented by Lena Wertmueller. What does sex have to do with the ability to rule by force?

2. What can you say about using rape as a metaphor for revolution?

3. What is the author's attitude toward sexual conquest—is it gender-based or not?

SAMPLE QUESTIONS FROM GLORIA GIBSON

El Norte (1984)

Beginning in the remote jungles of Guatemala, this highly acclaimed drama follows a brother and sister as they seek a better life in the "promised land." As they travel to the north (El Norte) courage and perseverance sustain them through the perilous journey. However, the two young Indians discover that the good life has its problems.

1. What are the Guatemalans' concept of the "good life" in America?

2. How is their journey similar to the "flight" of other oppressed people?

3. What is the significance of the sister's dying words?

4. How can this statement be compared with the earlier concept of the "good life?"

So Far from India (1982)

Ashok Sheth is an Indian immigrant who has come to New York to seek a better life for his family. Once there, he postpones sending for them. While in America, he grows away from the traditional life. Back in India, his despondent wife is forced to depend on her in-laws for sustenance. Tension mounts when Ashok returns to India to confront the situation.

1. What is Ashok's sisters' concept of the "good life?" How are their views different from Ashok's view?

2. What role does sexism play in the relationship between Ashok and his wife? What is her concept of the "good life"?

From Sun Up (1988)

This story of Tanzanian women in Africa documents their daily struggles. From dusk to dawn, they endure almost unbearable conditions, as they strive to make a life for themselves and their children. However, this is not a film of despair. *From Sun Up* dramatically illustrates that the women have hope in the realization that their future lies in the women's support of one another.

1. How is the concept of the "good life" in this film similar to and different from that in the other films?

2. What survival techniques have the women developed to cope with their situation?

3. What role does sexism play in determining the societal status of women?

General Questions

1. According to Juliet E. K. Walker, structural violence distinguishes the African American experience. Discuss the relevance of this statement in relationship to the films analyzed in the essay.

2. What does the term female-centered narrative mean? In what ways can films discussed in this essay be characterized as female-centered?

3. Discuss the differences and similarities of the films in regard to content and structure. What other films have you seen that address issues of violence and war? How would you compare them to the films in this essay?

4. Do you feel that violence against women and children has diminished in America or throughout the world? Do you feel that basic information about domestic violence has improved? In what ways does watching films like these help?

SAMPLE QUESTIONS FROM JOHN LOVELL

Hearts and Minds

Two years in the making, this film, produced by Bert Schneider and directed by Peter Davis, won an award at the 1974 Cannes Film Festival. It is a documentary, but not in the popular sense of simply providing an "impartial" record of events. Rather, it is a documentary with a point of view—an angry film, which has led some viewers to complain of its "bias." To reject the film out of hand, however, would be to miss the opportunity that the film provides for gaining insight into the sense of outrage that became widespread among Americans in the 1970s.

Moreover, the film is valuable in demonstrating that the Vietnam War had many victims—not just the soldiers killed in battle. Some of the most powerful moments in the film are associated with interviews conducted with both individuals who were in positions to influence policy and those in more humble roles. As you watch the film, pay particular attention to their experiences and their sentiments.

Randy Floyd	Navy Lt. George Coker
David and Mary Emerson	William Marshall
Edward Sowder	Robert Mueller
Daniel Ellsberg	Clark Clifford
J. William Fulbright	Walt W. Rostow

1. What was "the Vietnam War," in the minds of these characters? How do you explain any important similarities or differences in reactions?

2. What are the most powerful lessons about American national security policy to be learned from these individuals? All in all, do you think these lessons are well embedded or have we forgotten what we should have learned about Vietnam?

Doctor Strangelove; or How I Learned to Stop Worrying and Love the Bomb

To fully appreciate this film, it is necessary to have some familiarity with the Cold War "mindset" and with some of the characters who contributed to this mode of thinking.

Advice: Be attentive to zany detail—for example, the erotic symbolism of the in-flight refueling of the B-52; the Orwellian use of language of peace/war; the centerfold in a *Foreign Affairs* cover; the lyrics of the ballad "We'll Meet Again" sung as the mushroom cloud appears.

With reference to the list below,

1. What is each character's reaction to the events?
2. Is the playwright making a satirical point with the behavior of each character? If so, what?
3. Is this just good fun, or are there any lessons we should learn from the film?

Major King Kong (Slim Pickens)
Gen. Jack D. Ripper (Sterling Hayden)
Gp. Cpt. L. Mandrake (Peter Sellers)
Gen. Buck Turgidson (Geo. C. Scott)
Pres. Merlin Muffley (P. Sellers)

Dr. Strangelove (P. Sellers)
Miss Scott (Tracy Reed)
Col. Bat Guana (Keenan Wynn)
Amb. de Sadesky (P. Bull)
Lt. L. Zogg (James Earl Jones)

9

A Bibliographic Essay on Using Film to Teach about Peace Studies and Structural Violence

Kristine R. Brancolini

INTRODUCTION

The development of a film-based course requires only one resource—films! The films may be shown on 16mm film or on videocassette or laser disc. However, many published resources are available to help faculty select films, select required and supplemental readings, and develop assignments, learning activities, and lectures. Ideally, all faculty would have access to excellent film studies collections for both curriculum support and faculty research. These well-funded collections would include books, journals, and films on a variety of video formats, primarily videocassette and laser disc. All faculty would have a film studies librarian, knowledgeable about these collections and willing to add needed titles that are not already held by the library. Interlibrary loan would supplement local collections with more specialized scholarly materials. Computer services would allow easy access to the Internet, with its myriad human and electronic resources. However, most faculty develop courses under less than optimal conditions with regard to library resources. Many colleges and universities do not provide adequate library support for film studies. Many of the most prestigious universities still do not purchase video recordings, or they purchase only documentaries and other educational titles, excluding feature films on video. Video recordings are generally not available on interlibrary loan. Internet access may not be available, or your computer may not allow World Wide Web browsing. Given the print-oriented bias of most libraries, you will probably find many more books and journals on film than films and video recordings.

The purpose of the following chapter is to help you work within the framework of your local situation to find print and film and video resources to support your film course. You should begin by consulting a librarian—your film studies librarian (subject specialist), your media librarian (format specialist), a collection development librarian, or a general reference librarian. Depending upon your librarian's level of expertise and the depth and breadth of your film studies print collection and video collection, you may rely on this chapter more or less heavily to locate needed resources. If your local library is weak in the area of film studies or video collections, you can use the information in this chapter to make suggestions to your library or obtain materials from other sources. And if you have access to the Internet and World Wide Web, you may be able to overcome some of the deficiencies of your local collections and other resources.

LEARNING ABOUT FILMS

Faculty who want to develop a film-based course face two challenges, selecting titles to use and then locating those films on 16mm or video. Fortunately, many resources exist to help you accomplish both of these tasks. You will also want to read about these films, in books, journals, or in some electronic format.

The following resources fall into a number of categories, organized according to the order in which you will probably be using them. When developing a film course, most faculty begin with a few films that will definitely be included; however, you may also be searching for other films to use. The following reference books and the books in the Selected Bibliography near the end of this chapter were chosen because they represent the vast literature that deals with using film to teach concepts from other disciplines. This bibliography includes Library of Congress subject headings to help you assess the content of each book and to facilitate finding books in your local collections on the same subject. Books unavailable locally might be borrowed on interlibrary loan or requested for purchase for your local collection. These books are most likely to be found in your library's circulating collection. The resources listed under the various categories that follow are more likely to be found in your library's reference collection.

The resources for identifying films and video recordings that you might want to teach in your course or use as supplemental viewing include books, electronic databases, listservs, and other Internet resources. Some of these resources can also be used to help you learn more about the films you are considering for your course. The following annotated bibliographies will facilitate your search.

FEATURE FILMS ON VIDEO

The advantage of using feature films over educational films is that there is a thriving consumer market for feature films on video. Consequently, there are numerous consumer-oriented film lists that faculty can use to identify feature films on particular topics. Most of these books contain only very brief title entries; the emphasis is on categorizing the films. For more complete information about a particular film, consult the latest edition of one of the more general film guides, such as *Roger Ebert's Video Companion* (Kansas City, MO: Andrews and McNeel), *Leonard Maltin's Movie and Video Guide* (New York: Penguin Group), or *Halliwell's Film Guide* (New York: HarperCollins).

Arany, Lynne; Dyja, Tom; and Goldsmith, Gary. *The Reel List: A Categorical Companion to Over 2,000 Memorable Films.* New York: Dell, 1995. The authors' purpose is "to create a companion for the general reader and movie cultist alike, a companion that sorts movies into relatively uncommon categories, making connections, distinctions, and a host of associations" (Authors' Note, p. ix). Although the book was compiled with the home viewer in mind, many of the categories will help faculty find films that may serve an academic purpose. The entries are selective rather than comprehensive. An extensive section on history includes World War I, The Great Depression, World War II: Europe and the Atlantic, World War II: The Pacific and Elsewhere, World War II: The Homefront, Korea: The Forgotten War, The Red Menace, Black in America, and many more. This is one of the best film list books, simply because it makes unusual connections and identifies films that might be omitted from someone else's categorization.

Armstrong, Richard B.; and Armstrong, Mary Willems. *The Movie List Book: Hundreds of Fun and Fascinating Lists of Films by Their Settings and Major Themes.* 2d ed. Cincinnati: Betterway Books, 1994. Armstrong and Armstrong have defined over 550 categories, ranging from film themes and series to settings, occupations, animals, and happenstances. Each entry consists of a narrative, explaining the definition of the category, and a list of film titles with year of release. Films are listed in chronological order. The narrative presents a historic overview of the category or subcategory, highlighting notable films in the category. This book attempts comprehensiveness, particularly for film series. Consequently, very large categories were excluded, such as the Civil War and

World War II. The Korean War and Vietnam were included because there are relatively few films on these wars. Some categories you may find helpful include Atomic Bombs, Invasions/Takeovers of the U.S., Korean War, Ku Klux Klan, Labor Unions and Strikes, Lynching, and Vietnam.

Hiatt, Sky. *Picture This! A Guide to Over 300 Environmentally and Politically Relevant Films and Videos.* Chicago: The Noble Press, 1992. Hiatt hopes watching these films will trigger political action. Although its intended audience is unclear, this book has a much more serious purpose than simply providing for an evening's entertainment. These films were carefully selected and come highly recommended. For each film, Hiatt includes complete production information, a page-long review, and at least one other recommended title on the same topic. Appendices include a list of films; a subject index, with entries under Anti-Semitism, Capitalism, McCarthyism/Anti-Communism, Poverty, Revolution/Theory, among many others; a director index, and a source list. Hiatt reviews both well-known and obscure films, feature-length fiction and documentary films.

Lopez, Daniel. *Films by Genre.* Jefferson, NC: McFarland and Company, 1993. Here Lopez defines 775 categories, styles, trends, and movements, with a filmography for each. His list of films differs significantly from those in most of the other books discussed in this section. Like the other authors, Lopez is concerned with categorizing films, but he writes for a different audience and with a different purpose. First, he is writing primarily for the academic film scholar. The emphasis is on the definition of each genre; representative lists of films follow the definition. Second, many of the films listed in this book are not available on videocassette or laser disc. Thus, it is more a reference book than a viewing guide. It contains many more foreign films that any of the other sources, many of which are unavailable in the United States. However, it is a useful additional source of possible titles in a subject area. Some useful genres include Black Genre Movies, Conspiracy Film, Documentary (with numerous subgenres), Holocaust Film, Labor Film, Political Film, Revolutionary Film, Social Consciousness Film, and War Film (with numerous subgenres).

Wiener, Tom. *The Book of Video Lists.* 5th ed. Kansas City, MO: Andrews and McMeel, 1993. Weiner's goal also is to aid the perplexed video rental store patron, with more than 700 categories of films on videocassette, cross-referenced with 7,500 capsule reviews. He wants the reader to "think of this book as a video matchmaker, designed to get you and the right movie together for an evening's entertainment" (Introduction, p. vii). This book includes selective subject lists and comprehensive check lists (Director Check Lists, Writer Check Lists). With so many categories and subcategories, it must be browsed to be used effectively. Under the broad subject heading Action/Adventure, Weiner lists World War II, World War I, the Korean War, and the Vietnam War and its aftermath. Under Classics, he lists Social Problem Dramas; under Drama, Modern Problems, Family Crises, Troubled Youth, Today's Woman, Black Life, Political Dramas, and Strangers in Strange Lands: Tales of Culture Clash. More comprehensive than *The Reel List* (Arany et al), *The Book of Movie Lists* provides a valuable complement to that book.

DOCUMENTARY FILM AND VIDEO

Reference guides and lists of short documentary films intended for the educational market are less abundant. However, the resources listed below offer a starting point. Fortunately, these types of films and videos are more likely to be available in academic library collections and media centers, so you may find that local resources meet your needs. If not, these sources will help you find titles to rent or request for purchase.

National Video Resources (NVR) is an initiative of the Rockefeller Foundation dedicated to increasing the public's access to quality independent works on videocassette and other formats. The organization works with librarians and teaching faculty to raise awareness concerning these films through publications and workshops. Working with the John D. and Catherine T. MacArthur Foundation Library Project, NVR has published three *VideoForum* resource guides, one on Native Americans (1993), one on Latinos (1994), and one on health issues (1995). NVR has also received funding to publish a fourth *VideoForum* on understanding race. These publications are available from NVR, 73 Spring Street, Suite 606, New York, NY 10012 (212/274–8080). They are also available in many libraries. For more information about the work of NVR, contact them at the above address or telephone number, or by e-mail: NVRInfo@NVR.org.

Media Network (39 W. 14th Street, Suite 403, New York, NY 10011, 212/929–2663) publishes a series of film and video guides. Since 1979, Media Network has advocated and promoted use of independent film and video by activists, educators, libraries, and grassroots groups. Media Network publishes biannual media guides that identify the best media on social issues. Each entry includes production information, a review (approximately 150 to 200 words), and purchase information. Each guide has a subject index, an audience index, and a title index. A complete list of media guides appears as an appendix to this chapter.

Mediating History: The MAP [Media Alternatives Project] Guide to Independent Video by and about African American, Asian American, Latino, and Native American People, edited by Barbara Abrash and Catherine Egan

(New York: New York University Press, 1992), provides a selective, annotated videography useful in teaching American history. Film scholars have written accompanying essays that "identify important themes and issues, and ways of introducing independently-produced media into history teaching" (Introduction, p. 3). Kimberly Everett contributes "Alternative Media Resources: A Guide." There are also title, subject, and chronological indexes.

A third useful resource is *The Third World in Film and Video, 1984–1990*, by Helen W. Cyr (Metuchen, NJ: Scarecrow, 1991), which updates *A Filmography of the Third World* (1976) and *A Filmography of the Third World, 1976–1983* (1985) from the same author and publisher. Cyr provides production information and a brief annotation for over 1,100 documentary films and videos. Organized by the country that is the subject of the film or video, the book includes a list of distributors and a title index.

LISTSERVS AND OTHER INTERNET RESOURCES

Often, the best resource is a human resource. Listservs enable you to consult with hundreds of experts simultaneously and internationally. Subscribers to listservs can answer all sorts of questions: suggest films on a particular topic, recommend sources of films, identify experts on a subject who might be willing to communicate with you. Two of the best listservs for film studies are H-Film and Screen-L. H-Film is moderated by Steven Mintz of the History Department at the University of Houston. It is an "international scholarly forum to promote the scholarly study of film, television, radio and the use of film and videotape in teaching. . . . The primary purpose of H-Film is to enable scholars to communicate their current research and teaching interests and test new ideas" (from the "Welcome to H-Film" message). To subscribe, send this e-mail message to listserv@uicvm.uic.edu (Internet) or listserv@uicvm (Bitnet): sub H-Film <yourname>. Leave the subject line blank. Screen-L is moderated by Jeremy Butler of the Department of Telecommunications and Film at the University of Alabama, Tuskaloosa. "Screen-L is designed for persons teaching, researching, and making film and television—whether they are film/TV educators, students, professionals, media librarians, or self-schooled fans. Discussion, therefore, is invited regarding film/TV criticism, theory, history, production issues, and teaching" (from the "You are now subscribed to SCREEN-L" message). To subscribe, send the same subscription message above to listserv@ua1vm.ua.edu (Internet). Again, leave the subject line blank.

There are also a number of useful and interesting World Wide Web meta sites for film and television studies. Meta sites are large websites that attempt to link all relevant websites on a particular subject. Using these sites, you will be able to locate hundreds of useful websites.

CineMedia, American Film Institute

> http://www.afionline.org/CineMedia/cmframe.html

Media and Communications Studies (Film Studies), University of Wales, Aberystwyth

> http://www.aber.ca.uk/~dgc/media.html

Mega Media Links, Northwestern University

> http://omnibus-eye.rtvf.nwu/links/main-menu.html

SCREENsite: Film and TV Studies, University of Alabama

> http://www.sa.ua.edu/TCF/contents.html

WebOvision (Film & Theatre)

> http://www.webovision.com/cgibin/var/media/sd/film.html

FILM REVIEWS: FULL-TEXT AND INDEXES

Many of the works used to identify films and videos by subject provide only brief evaluative information, if any. However, there are numerous sources of film reviews and critical articles on films. Many of these are print sources and should be listed in your library's catalog. As reference books, however, most will be noncirculating and not available on interlibrary loan. Some of these sources are CD-ROM databases, so check with your library's reference department for availability; they may or may not be listed in your library's catalog. The online sources, described as "computer files," are most likely to be found on your library's computer system. You can access the Internet database on your own. However, to be sure, consult a librarian. In general, reviews to older films will be found in print sources; reviews to more recent films will be found in computer-based resources. *Film Literature Index* and *Media Review Digest* represent notable exceptions to this generalization.

Batty, Linda. *Retrospective Index to Film Periodicals, 1930–1971.* New York: Bowker, 1975. Batty indexes fourteen film journals plus the film reviews and articles from the *Village Voice* from the beginning of each journal through 1971.

Bowles, Stephen E. *Index to Critical Film Reviews in British and American Film Periodicals*, together with *Index to Critical Reviews of Books about*

Film, 1930–1972. 2 vols. New York: B. Franklin, 1974–75. Bowles primarily indexes reviews of theatrical fiction films, but also includes some documentary, experimental, short and educational films.

Expanded Academic Index (InfoTrac). Belmont, CA: Information Access. Computer file. This online source indexes articles analyzing films and film reviews by title, from 1980 to the present.

Film Index International. Alexandria, VA: Chadwyck-Healey, Inc. CD-ROM. *Film Index International* provides information on 90,000 feature films and 30,000 personalities. Each film entry includes a brief synopsis of the film, complete cast information, and production information. Under each film title a function key takes users to a list of citations of film reviews and scholarly articles about the film. This is a product of the British Film Institute; consequently, it has the best coverage of foreign films to be found in a film database.

Film Literature Index: A Quarterly Author-Subject Periodical Index to the International Literature of Film. Albany, NY: Film & Documentation Center, State University of New York at Albany. This quarterly index, cumulated annually, provides subject access to over 300 international film periodicals. *Film Literature Index* encompasses critical articles on films as well as reviews of films.

Film Review Annual. Englewood Cliffs, NJ: J.S. Ozer. This source compiles full-text reviews of feature films released in the United States. Citations are provided for additional reviews.

General Periodicals Index (InfoTrac). Belmont, CA: Information Access. Computer file. This online index provides access to reviews by title, subject, director, and major performers. Entries are graded (A, B, C, etc.) to indicate the reviewer's judgment.

The Internet Movie Database. http://us.imdb.com. The full-text reviews in this database come from a variety of published sources—magazines, newspapers, and arts magazines, and from individual reviewers; you can even add your own reviews! The published sources include *Entertainment Weekly, Time Magazine, San Francisco Chronicle*, and *eye WEEKLY*, an arts newspaper published in Toronto. This database is most useful in locating reviews of films in current release; once films have left theaters, they are less likely to be represented. However, it is also a reference tool, providing an unbelievable wealth of information about performers and directors, which can be used to create filmographies.

Magill's Survey of Cinema. Peabody, MA: EBSCO Publishing. CD-ROM. This is a CD-ROM version of *Magill's Survey of Cinema* (1980–1985) and *Magill's Cinema Annual*, including English-language films, foreign-language films, and silent films. The database can be searched by film title, keyword, or phrase. Highly selective, *Magill's* includes full-text reviews and storyline summaries for over 4,000 films and citations to other reviews. *Magill's* also notes whether a film is available on videocassette.

Media Review Digest. Ann Arbor, MI: Pierian Press. This is an annual index to reviews, evaluations, and descriptions of non-book media appearing in a variety of periodicals and reviewing sources. The Film and Video section lists reviews of both educational films and feature films. Symbols summarize the reviewer's evaluation (+ or -); an asterisked entry (*) indicates a descriptive, nonevaluative article. This is the only compilation of reviews for educational films; all other sources on this list publish reviews or compile reviews for feature films.

Microsoft Cinemania: Interactive Movie Guide. Redmond, WA: Microsoft. Although designed for the home multimedia market, *Cinemania* is actually a hybrid movie finder and reference source that appeals to both the home-video viewer and the academic user. Updated annually, the 1995 edition includes 19,000 feature films, with multiple reviews for many of them. Full-text reviews are contributed by Leonard Maltin (starred evaluation with a very short review for each film), Roger Ebert, Pauline Kael, and reviewers from CineBooks' *Motion Picture Guide* (for selected films). The latest edition can also be searched topically through a feature called "Cinemania Suggests."

Motion Picture Guide. New York: CineBooks. CD-ROM. The CD-ROM version of *The Motion Picture Guide* and *Motion Picture Guide Annual* contains full-text reviews of nearly 30,000 sound films released in the United States between 1927 and 1994. Although the print version does not offer as many search options, the CD-ROM version omits the name of the reviewer. Nevertheless, this is an extremely authoritative and reliable source of reviews.

New York Times Film Reviews. New York: New York Times. This source reprints full-text reviews published in the *New York Times*. Volume 6 is the index to vols. 1–5 (1913–1968); biennial supplements after 1968 update the compilation.

Variety Film Reviews, 1907–1986. New York: Garland, 1983–1988. Like the *New York Times Film Reviews*, this is a full-text compilation of film reviews published in *Variety*. Only feature length films are included after 1927.

LOCATING FEATURE FILMS AND DOCUMENTARY FILMS ON VIDEO—LOCAL SOURCES

Once you have selected the films and videos you would like to use in class or for supplemental viewing, you have a number of alternatives for actually obtaining these materials. The feature film market is largely consumer-driven, so there are many more sources of feature films on videotape and laser disc than there are for documentary and educational films. Some documentaries with broad appeal, beyond an academic setting, are released on home video. These will be advertised in the same sources as feature films and may be easier to locate. However, most documentary films are available only through educational distributors. These films are likely to be accessible only through college or university-related channels, such as the library or campus media center.

College or University Library

Most academic libraries collect feature films and documentaries on videocassette and/or laser disc. However, collections tend to be small even at large universities. Explore your library's video collection. If your library does not have the titles you want, request that the librarian buy them. The person responsible for the selection of video may be one media librarian or may be several subject bibliographers. If your library does not have a video collection, discuss the possibility of establishing one with the director of your library. All academic libraries should be collecting video recordings.

College or University Media Center

Many academic institutions separate media collections from library collections. Others have two film and video collections, one in a media center and one in the library. Academic libraries usually began developing motion picture collections with the advent of videocassette, leaving the collection of 16mm film to other administrative units on campus. Over time, the 16mm rental collections often expanded into the collection of videocassettes. Consequently, you may find one 16mm film collection on campus, but two video collections. Or your library may not collect video recordings at all, leaving the purchase of all motion pictures to the media center.

Public Library

Some public libraries have extensive collections of videocassettes and laser discs. Familiarize yourself with your public library's video collection. If you live in a metropolitan area, you may find that your public library's video collection is vastly superior to that of your college or university library. Even in medium-sized cities, some public libraries have focused their video collection-building in the area of independent and foreign films, making them excellent sources of obscure films.

Video Rental Stores

Video rental stores offer an alternative source of feature films and documentaries released for the home market. Visit each one in your community, noting which have the best collections for your purposes. There are also national rental sources, which will be discussed in the next section. People may tell you that video recordings rented from video stores may not be used in the classroom; however, this is false. The face-to-face teaching exemption of the copyright law allows the use of home video in the classroom. Nothing in the law excludes video recordings that have been rented. (See the section on copyright below.)

Interlibrary Loan

Some libraries have begun lending their videocassettes on interlibrary loan. While this practice is not widespread, some colleges and universities have reciprocal borrowing agreements with other institutions in the state or within the region. For example, the eight campuses of Indiana University Libraries lend to one another and within the Committee on Inter-Institutional Cooperation (CIC), the universities of the Big 10, plus the University of Chicago. You should not overlook the possibility of borrowing video recordings through interlibrary loan.

FINDING DISTRIBUTORS AND RENTAL SOURCES

Once you have checked local sources and determined that films you want to use are not available from one of the sources listed above, the following reference books will help you determine whether or not a particular film you want to use has been released on video. While there is no "video recordings in print," together, these four sources provide the best information about video recordings that may be purchased. Some also include rental availability and prices.

Feature Films on Video—Purchase

Bowker's Complete Video Directory. New York: R.R. Bowker. Vol. 1: Entertainment, Vols. 2 and 3: Educational/Special Interest. (Annual; supplements issued irregularly.) Volume 1 includes feature films and performances. All 37,000 titles listed in the 1993 edition are in active distribution, have home-viewing rights, and are priced for the home market. Descriptive and ordering information is presented for each title. Separate indexes list video recordings by title, genre, cast/director, awards, Spanish language, laser videodisc, and more. Each entry includes a brief summary. There is also a CD-ROM version of this reference source, *Variety's Complete Video Directory Plus*, that includes all of the same information, searchable more ways, plus full-text reviews from *Variety*.

OCLC/FirstSearch/WorldCat. WorldCat is a database created by librarians sharing their cataloging efforts. Until recently, the only way to search OCLC/WorldCat was through awkward search keys; it was not meant to be used as a reference tool by public service librarians or by library users. The situation has now changed for the better. FirstSearch provides access to numerous databases using simple command language similar to that used to search a local online library catalog. WorldCat gathers catalog records from thousands of libraries around the world, including millions of records for audiovisual materials. At some universities, FirstSearch/WorldCat are menu choices on the library's online catalog system. It can be searched most of the ways you can search your own library's system—by author, by title, by keyword, and by subject. More importantly, you can also limit your search in a number of ways—by type of material ("media," for video recordings and films), by date, and by other qualifiers.

Video Source Book. Detroit: Gale Research. 2 vols. (Annual; supplements in February and June.) Like the Bowker source described above, the *Video Source Book* attempts to provide a comprehensive listing of videos-in-print. It lists and describes more than 127,000 programs currently available on video from nearly 1700 sources and includes starred evaluations for feature films and short descriptions. Prices are given for most home video titles. Although they purport to cover the same releases, it is necessary to consult both *Bowker's Complete Video Directory* and the *Video Source Book*, as they frequently do not overlap.

Videolog. San Diego, CA: Trade Service Corporation. (Weekly.) *Videolog* offers only a very brief description of each title, but because it is updated and issued weekly (looseleaf service), it most accurately reflects which films are available on videocassette or laser videodisc. *Videolog* is available in many video stores as well as libraries. It is also available on CD-ROM.

Feature Films on Video—Rental

The best known and probably the most useful mail-order video rental source for academic purposes is Facets, "the nation's largest library of foreign, classic and independent films" (according to their catalog), located in Chicago. Facets sells videocassettes and laser discs, but they also rent through the mail. Facets publishes a catalog listing of over 22,000 tapes in their collection. To obtain a catalog or learn more about their services, contact Facets at 800/832–2387.

16mm Film Rentals

The use of 16mm film is declining, even in film studies courses. As prints wear out, many film rental companies are not replacing them. Film studies departments complain that the quality of the prints is deteriorating. However, 16mm is the preferred format for large-group showings, even with the proliferation of video projection equipment. Most departments rely on rental for these films. Film rental sources include both commercial and not-for-profit university-based collections. The university collections have educational films exclusively; you will be able to locate many documentaries and supplemental films in these collections. They are dramatically less expensive to rent than those from commercial sources. These film rental operations also rent video recordings, although your local library or media center is more likely to have relevant video recordings.

The two primary reference books on 16mm film rental are *Film Programmer's Guide to 16mm Rentals*, 3d ed., edited by Kathleen Weaver (Albany, CA: Reel Research, 1980) and *Feature Films: A Directory of Feature Films on 16mm and Videotape Available for Rental, Sale, and Lease*, 8th ed., by James L. Limbacher (New York: Bowker, 1985). Although these sources are now more than ten years old, they still offer the only compilations of this information. Three major companies supply most film rentals: Films, Inc., New Yorker Films, and Swank. If you will be renting 16mm films or exploring the possibility of doing so, you will want to receive current catalogs from all three companies:

Films, Inc. 4447 N. Ravenswood, Chicago, IL 60640.800/323–4222. The Entertainment Division of Public Media/Films, Inc., distributes feature films on 16mm and 35mm and public performance video. They are the exclusive nontheatrical distributor for thousands of films from several Hollywood and independent producers, including Paramount Pictures, New Line Cinema, Twentieth Century Fox, Fine Line Features, Columbia Pictures, Savoy Pictures, TriStar Pictures, and Northern Arts Entertainment. Classroom rates range between $75 and $400 and vary depending upon the age, popularity, and royalty rate for the title. PMI/Films, Inc., offers quantity discounts for orders of three or more films (letter from Marc McClellan, Senior Accounts Manager, May 31, 1995).

New Yorker Films, 16 West 61st Street, New York, NY 10023.212/247–6110. New Yorker Films distributes the work of many well-known international filmmakers, on 35mm, 16mm, and video (phone conversation with Stephen Wolfe,

June 1, 1995). They rent for nontheatrical and theatrical use, with a different pricing structure depending upon the use. Terms are available for multiple showings and for small film societies. Their catalogs list rental prices for non-theatrical, nontelevision use, but they offer classroom rates as well. New Yorker specializes in the work of critically acclaimed directors, both established and emerging.

Swank Motion Pictures, Inc., 910 Riverside, Elmhurst, IL 60126.800/876–3330. Swank Motion Pictures, Inc., is a nontheatrical film and video distributor supplying colleges and universities in the United States with "the largest collection of movies from Hollywood's top studios" (letter from Maureen Nosek, May 31, 1995). Swank is the exclusive distributor for Universal, Walt Disney, Warner Brothers, Touchstone, Miramax, Hollywood, United Artists, MGM, and Orion. The rental fee depends upon the title and the format. Films are available on 36mm, 16mm, and video formats. Package pricing is available on orders of four or more films.

The members of the Consortium of College and University Media Centers (CCUMC) rent educational film and video; they gather the resources of all member collections into a reference book, *Educational Film and Video Locator* (New York: Bowker, 1991), which is now available on CD-ROM, as *Media-Source One*. The collections represented in the *Educational Film and Video Locator* offer an inexpensive alternative to commercial rental sources. However, many of these collections are closing their operations or changing their focus from national rental to local service.

COPYRIGHT

Most feature films on video will be licensed for home use only, and these words will appear somewhere on the box and on the videocassette itself. The Copyright Law of 1976 allows teachers to use these videocassettes in face-to-face teaching (known as "The Face-to-Face Teaching Exemption"). Most copyright experts agree that the Fair Use Doctrine also permits viewing of these videocassettes in a library media center. However, it is illegal to duplicate these commercially acquired video recordings for your own collection, to use in class, or for the library to build its collection.

The Off-Air Taping Guidelines that accompany the Copyright Law stipulate the conditions under which educators may videotape broadcasts off-air or off-cable. The ruling in the Sony Betamax case allows individuals to tape off-air for their own private use. However, these recordings may be used in the classroom only under strict conditions, with time limits. Teachers may not bring their own privately recorded videotapes into their classrooms unless they meet the requirements of the guidelines. If legal video recordings are available, they will provide your students with vastly superior viewing experiences. However, the film you want to use may never have been released on video. The copyright holder retains this legal right, and if the film you want to use has not been released on video, you may not use it with your students; you must select another film.

CONCLUSIONS

Faculty who want to develop a film-based course face challenges to locating print and nonprint resources. Academic institutions offer an uneven array of audiovisual collections and services. Consequently, you may find it easier to read about films than to view them! The situation is changing, however; and by working with librarians and other media specialists, you should be able to assemble the necessary print and nonprint resources to offer your students a superior film-based learning opportunity.

SELECTED BIBLIOGRAPHY

The books in this selected bibliography represent some of the most useful works available on using film to teach disciplines other than film studies. The Library of Congress subject headings are included to help you find other books on the same subjects in your local library. When a book has been published in more than one edition, only the latest edition has been listed.

Aldgate, Anthony, and Richards, Jeffrey. *Britain Can Take It: The British Cinema in the Second World War.* 2d ed. Edinburgh: Edinburgh University Press, 1994. Subject headings: World War, 1939–1945—Motion pictures and the war; Motion pictures—Great Britain—History.

American History/American Film: Interpreting the Hollywood Image. Edited by John E. O'Connor and Martin A. Jackson. Expanded and updated. New York: Ungar, 1988. Subject headings: Motion pictures—United States—History; Motion pictures and history; United States—Civilization—Sources.

Avisar, Ilan. *Screening the Holocaust: Cinema's Images of the Unimaginable.* Bloomington: Indiana University Press, 1988. Subject heading: Holocaust, Jewish (1939–1945), in motion pictures.

Belton, John. *American Cinema/American Culture.* New York: McGraw-Hill, 1994. Subject headings: Motion pictures—United States—History; Motion picture industry—United States—History. Motion pictures—Social aspects—United States; Popular culture—United States—History—20th century.

Biskind, Peter. *Seeing Is Believing: How Hollywood Taught Us to Stop Worrying and Love the Fifties.* New York: Pantheon Books, 1983. Subject headings: Motion pictures—Political aspects—United States; Motion pictures—United States—History.

Blake, Richard Aloysius. *Screening America: Reflections on Five Classic Films.* New York: Paulist Press, 1991. Subject headings: Film criticism; Motion pictures—United States—Reviews.

Celluloid Power: Social Film Criticism from the Birth of a Nation *to* Judgment at Nuremberg. Edited by David Platt. Metuchen, NJ: Scarecrow Press, 1992. Subject headings: Politics in motion pictures; Motion pictures—Political aspects; Motion pictures—History; Motion pictures—Reviews.

Christensen, Terry. *Reel Politics: American Political Movies from* Birth of a Nation *to* Platoon. Oxford, England, and New York: Blackwell, 1987. Subject headings: Motion pictures—Political aspects—United States; Politics in motion pictures; Motion pictures—United States—History.

Colombat, Andre. *The Holocaust in French Film.* Metuchen, NJ: Scarecrow Press, 1993. Subject headings: Holocaust, Jewish (1939–1945), in motion pictures; Motion pictures—France—History.

Colonialism and Nationalism in Asian Cinema. Edited by Wimal Dissanayake. Bloomington: Indiana University Press, 1994. Subject headings: Motion pictures—Asia; Motion pictures—Political aspects—Asia.

Combs, James E. *American Political Movies: An Annotated Filmography of Feature Films.* New York: Garland, 1990. Subject headings: Politics in motion pictures—Catalogs; Motion pictures—Political aspects—United States.

Combs, James E., and Combs, Sara T. *Film Propaganda and American Politics: An Analysis and Filmography.* New York: Garland, 1994. Subject headings: Motion pictures in propaganda—United States—History; Politics in motion pictures; Motion pictures—Political aspects—United States; Advertising, Political—United States.

Considine, David M. *The Cinema of Adolescence.* Jefferson, NC: McFarland, 1985. Subject headings: Youth in motion pictures; Motion pictures and youth; Social problems in motion pictures.

Devine, Jeremy M. *Vietnam at 24 Frames a Second: A Critical and Thematic Analysis of Over 350 Films about the Vietnam War.* Jefferson, NC: McFarland, 1995. Subject headings: Vietnamese Conflict, 1961–1975—Motion pictures and the conflict, Indochinese War; 1946–1954—Motion pictures and the war; War films—United States—History and criticism.

Doherty, Thomas Patrick. *Projections of War: Hollywood, American Culture, and World War II.* New York: Columbia University Press, 1993. Subject headings: World War, 1939–1945—Motion pictures and the war; Motion pictures—United States—History—20th century.

Doneson, Judith E. *The Holocaust in American Film.* Philadelphia: Jewish Publication Society, 1987. Subject headings: Holocaust, Jewish (1939–1945), in motion pictures; Antisemitism in motion pictures; Motion pictures—United States.

Ferro, Marc. *Cinema and History*. Translated by Naomi Greene. Detroit: Wayne State University Press, 1988. Subject heading: Motion pictures and history.

Film and Politics in the Third World. Edited by John D.H. Downing. New York: Praeger, 1987. Subject headings: Motion pictures—Developing countries; Motion pictures—Political aspects.

Film and the First World War. Edited by Karel Dibbets and Bert Hogenkamp. Amsterdam: Amsterdam University Press, 1995. Subject headings: World War, 1914–1918—Motion pictures and the war; Historical films—History and criticism; Motion pictures and history; Documentary films—History and criticism.

Fyne, Robert. *The Hollywood Propaganda of World War II*. Edited by Robert Fyne. Metuchen, NJ: Scarecrow Press, 1994. Subject headings: World War, 1939–1945—Propaganda; Propaganda, American; World War, 1939–1945—Motion pictures and the war; Motion pictures—United States—History—20th century.

Hollywood as Historian : American Film in a Cultural Context. Edited by Peter C. Rollins. Lexington, KY: University Press of Kentucky, c.1983. Subject headings: Historical films—United States—History and criticism; Motion pictures and history; Motion picture plays—History and criticism.

Insdorf, Annette. *Indelible Shadows: Film and the Holocaust*. 2d edition. Cambridge, England, and New York: Cambridge University Press, 1989. Subject heading: Holocaust, Jewish (1939–1945), in motion pictures.

Isenberg, Michael T. *War on Film: The American Cinema and World War I, 1914–1941*. Rutherford, NJ: Fairleigh Dickinson University Press, 1980. Subject headings: World War, 1914–1918, in motion pictures; Motion pictures and history; Documentary films—History and criticism; Historical films—History and criticism.

Jowett, Garth. *Film: The Democratic Art*. Boston: Little, Brown, 1976. Subject headings: Motion pictures—United States; Motion pictures—Social aspects.

Kaes, Anton. *From Hitler to Heimat: The Return of History as Film*. Rev. and enl. translation of: Deutschlandbilder. Cambridge, MA: Harvard University Press, 1989. Subject headings: Motion pictures—Germany (West)—History; Motion pictures producers and directors—Germany (West); Motion picture plays—History and criticism; Motion pictures and history.

Kenez, Peter. *Cinema and Soviet Society, 1917–1953*. Cambridge, England and New York: Cambridge University Press, 1992. Subject headings: Motion pictures—Political aspects—Soviet Union; Motion pictures—Soviet Union—History.

Lanning, Michael Lee. *Vietnam at the Movies*. 1st ed. New York: Fawcett Columbine, 1994. Subject headings: Vietnamese Conflict, 1961–1975—Motion pictures and the conflict; Motion pictures—United States—History.

Levy, Emmanuel. *Small-Town America in Film: The Decline and Fall of Community*. New York: Continuum, 1991. Subject headings: City and town life in motion pictures; United States in motion pictures.

MacBean, James Roy. *Film and Revolution*. Bloomington: Indiana University Press, c.1975. Subject headings: Motion pictures—Political aspects; Communism and motion pictures.

Michalczyk, John J. *The Italian Political Filmmakers*. Rutherford, NJ: Fairleigh Dickinson University Press, 1986. Subject headings: Motion pictures—Italy—History. Motion pictures—Political aspects—Italy—History.

Mulvey, Laura. *Visual and Other Pleasures*. Bloomington: Indiana University Press, 1989. Subject headings: Women in motion pictures; Motion pictures—Political aspects; Feminism.

Murray, Bruce Arthur. *Film and the German Left in the Weimar Republic: From Caligari to Kuhle Wumpe*. Austin: University of Texas Press, 1990. Subject headings: Motion pictures—Germany—History; Motion pictures—Political aspects—Germany.

Muse, Eben J. *The Land of Nam: The Vietnam War in American Film*. Metuchen, NJ: Scarecrow, 1994. Subject headings: Vietnamese Conflict, 1961–1975—Motion pictures and the conflict; Motion pictures—United States—History and criticism.

Nichols, Bill. *Blurred Boundaries: Questions of Meaning in Contemporary Culture*. Bloomington: Indiana University Press, 1994. Subject headings:Documentary films—History and criticism; Historical films—History and criticism; Motion pictures in ethnology.

Propaganda, Politics, and Film, 1918–45. Edited by Nicholas Pronay and D. W. Spring. London: Macmillan Press, 1982. Subject headings: Motion pictures in propaganda; Motion pictures—Political aspects; World War, 1939–1945—Motion pictures and the war; Motion pictures—Great Britain—History; Motion pictures—Soviet Union—History; Propaganda, British; Propaganda, Russian; World War, 1939–1945—Propaganda.

Quart, Leonard, and Auster, Albert. *American Film and Society since 1945*. 2d ed. New York: Praeger, 1991. Subject headings: Motion pictures—Social aspects—United States; Motion Pictures—United States—History; Social problems in motion pictures.

Rebhorn, Marlette. *Screening America: Using Hollywood Films to Teach History*. New York: P. Lang, 1988. Subject headings: Historical films—United States—History and criticism; United States in motion pictures; Motion pictures—United States—History; Motion pictures and history; United States—History—Study and teaching—Audio-visual aids.

The Red Screen: Politics, Society, Art in Soviet Cinema. Edited by Anna Lawton. New York: Routledge, 1992. Subject headings: Motion pictures—Soviet Union; Motion pictures—Political aspects—Soviet Union.

Revisioning History: Film and the Construction of a New Past. Edited by Robert Rosenstone. Princeton, NJ: Princeton University Press, 1995. Subject heading: Motion pictures and history.

Richards, Jeffrey and Aldgate, Anthony. *British Cinema and Society, 1930–1970.* Totowa, NJ: Barnes & Noble Books, 1983. Subject headings: Motion pictures and history; Motion picture plays—History and criticism; Motion pictures—Great Britain.

Ryan, Michael, and Kellner, Douglas. *Camera Politica: The Politics and Ideology of Contemporary Hollywood Film.* Bloomington: Indiana University Press, 1988. Subject heading: Motion pictures—Political aspects—United States.

Sarris, Andrew. *Politics and Cinema.* New York: Columbia University Press, 1978. Subject headings: Motion pictures—Political aspects; Motion pictures—Reviews.

Screening Europe: Image and Identity in Contemporary European Cinema. Edited by Duncan Petrie. London: British Film Institute, 1992. Subject headings: Motion pictures—Europe; Motion pictures—Social aspects—Europe; Motion pictures—Political aspects—Europe.

Skal, David J. *The Monster Show: A Cultural History of Horror.* New York: Norton, 1992. Subject headings: Horror films—History and criticism; Social problems in motion pictures.

Sklar, Robert. *Movie-Made America: A Social History of American Movies.* New York: Random House, 1975. Subject headings: Motion pictures—United States—History.

Sorlin, Pierre. *The Film in History: Restaging the Past.* Oxford, England: Blackwell, 1980. Subject headings: Motion pictures and history; Historical films—History and criticism.

White, David Manning, and Averson, Richards. *The Celluloid Weapon: Social Comment in the American Film.* Boston, Beacon Press, 1972. Subject headings: Social problems in motion pictures; Motion pictures—United States—History.

Wood, Robin. *Hollywood from Vietnam to Reagan.* New York: Columbia University Press, 1986. Subject headings: Motion pictures—United States—History; Motion picture plays—History and criticism; Motion pictures—Political aspects.

Zavarzadeh, Mas'ud. *Seeing Films Politically.* Albany: State University of New York Press, 1991. Subject headings: Motion pictures—Political aspects; Motion pictures—Philosophy.

APPENDIX 1

Media Resource Guides

Two organizations, National Video Resources and the Media Network, publish media guides that promote the use of independent film and video to teach about social issues. In addition to issuing publications, these organizations offer training and other support to educators who want to learn more about using film and video in the classroom or in other educational settings.

Media network publications:

In Her Own Image (1991). 82 films and videos on women and community development, with an international scope. Sections include Food, Clothing and Shelter; All Work and No Play; The Body Politic; War and Peace; Confronting Violence; Changing Roles; and Educate, Agitate, Organize!

A Reality Check on the American Dream: The Guide to Anti-Poverty Film and Video (1991). 75 films and videos on poverty-related issues, including neglected communities, education, healthcare, and anti-poverty organizing.

Choice: Women's Reproductive Freedom and Health (1990). 60 films and videos on topics such as reproductive health, childcare, birth control, abortion, gay and teenage sexuality, single mothers, and attacks on women's rights.

Bombs Aren't Cool (1989). More than 100 of the best films and videos on peace, disarmament, and militarism.

Images of Color (1989). More than 80 films and videos on issues affecting Asian-American, African-American, Latino and Native-American communities.

Safe Planet (1990). More than 60 films and videos addressing environmental issues and grassroots activism.

Seeing through AIDS (1989). More than 80 films and videos addressing AIDS and related issues, including women and AIDS, youth, and AIDS activism.

10

Filmography

Kristine R. Brancolini

All but one of the films on this list are available on video. The feature films are all available on home video in various releases. Check your college or university library first, then your public library. If not available at a local library, these video recordings can be purchased through any home video outlet, including video stores, discount stores, and catalogs. On the filmography below all home video titles have been noted as "Home video." The other films may also be available in a library, and they are all available for purchase on video, but from exclusive distributors. We have listed the distributor for these films; a list of distributor names and addresses follows this filmography.

The Accused. Dir. Jonathan Kaplan. Paramount, 1988. Home video.
All Quiet on the Western Front. Dir. Lewis Millstone. Universal, 1930. Home video.
The Americanization of Emily. Dir. Paddy Chayefsky. MGM, 1964. Home video.
And Still I Rise. Dir. Ngozi Onwurah. Non-Aligned Productions for BBC Television, 1991. Distributor, Women Make Movies, 1993.
Angel Heart. Dir. Alan Parker. Winkast/Union/Carolco, 1987. Home video.
Atomic Café. Dir. Kevin Rafferty, Jayne Loader, and Pierce Rafferty. Archives Project, 1982. Home video.
Basic Instinct. Dir. Paul Verhoeven. Carolco Pictures/Le Studio Canal, 1992. Home video.
Battle of Algiers [La Battaglia di Algeri]. Dir. Gillo Pontecorvo. Igor Films, 1966. Home video.

The Beginning or the End. Dir. Norman Taurog. MGM, 1947. Never released on
    video.
Born on the Fourth of July. Dir. Oliver Stone. Universal, 1989. Home video.
Burning Bed. Dir. Robert Greenwald. Tisch/Avnet Financial, 1985. Home video.
Cape Fear. Dir. J. Lee Thompson. Universal, 1962. Home video.
Cape Fear. Dir. Martin Scorsese. Universal and Amblin Entertainment, 1991.
    Home video.
Un Chien Andalou [Andalousian Dog]. Dir. Luis Bunuel. 1928. Released alone
    and on numerous compilation tapes of experimental films. Home video.
Daughters of the Dust. Dir. Julie Dash. American Playhouse Theatrical Films,
    1991. Home video.
"Dawn" (*War and Peace in the Nuclear Age series*). Distributor, Annenberg/CPB
    Project, 1988.
The Day after Trinity. Dir. Jon Else. Jon Else in association with KTEH, San Jose,
    1981. Distributors, Pyramid Films, 1981 (videocassette); Voyager, 1995
    (laser disc).
Dr. Strangelove; or, How I Learned to Stop Worrying and Love the Bomb. Dir.
    Stanley Kubrick. Columbia Pictures, 1963. Home video.
Do the Right Thing. Dir. Spike Lee. 40 Acres and a Mule, 1989. Home video.
"Dreamworlds." Dir. Sut Jhally. Media Education Foundation, 1990. Distributor,
    Media Education Foundation. The original "Dreamworlds" is now out-
    of-print, but an updated "Dreamworlds II" (1995) is available.
Enola Gay. Dir. Lowell Rich. 1980. Home video.
Faith Even to the Fire: Nuns for Social Justice. Sylvan Productions, 1991. Dis-
    tributor, Filmakers Library, 1991.
Fat Man and Little Boy. Dir. Roland Joffe. Paramount, 1989. Home video.
Fatal Attraction. Dir. Adrian Lyne. Paramount, 1987. Home video.
Gallipoli. Dir. Peter Weir. R&R Films PTY, Ltd., 1981. Home video.
Gandhi. Dir. Richard Attenborough. International Film Investors/Goldcrest/Indo-
    British Films/National Film Development, 1982. Home video.
Good Morning, Vietnam. Dir. Barry Levinson. Touchstone/Silver Partners III,
    1987. Home video.
The Grapes of Wrath. Dir. John Ford. Fox, 1940. Home video.
Greenham Challenge: Bringing Missiles to Trial. Dir. Peter Wiesner. Distributor,
    Wiesner Associates, 1987.
Hearts and Minds. Dir. Peter Davis. Rainbow Pictures, distributed by Warner
    Bros., 1975. Home video.
Heaven and Earth. Dir. Oliver Stone. Warner Bros., 1993. Home video.
Kumekucha: From Sun Up. Dir. Flora M'mbugu-Schelling. 1987. Distributor,
    Films for the Humanities and Sciences, 1992.
Maids and Madams. Dir. Mire Hamermesh. 1986. Distributor, Filmakers Library,
    1985, 1988.
Mississippi Burning. Dir. Alan Parker. Orion, 1988. Home video.

Mrs. Miniver. Dir. William Wyler. MGM, 1942. Home video.

The Nasty Girl. Dir. Michael Verhoeven. Miramax, 1990.

El Norte. Dir. Gregory Nava. Independent Productions; American Playhouse, 1983. Home video.

Official Story [La historia oficial]. Dir. Luis Puenzo. Almi Pictures, 1985. Home video.

Platoon. Dir. Oliver Stone. Hemdale, 1986. Home video.

Pretty Woman. Dir. Garry Marshall. Silver Screen Partners/Touchstone, 1990. Home video.

A Raisin in the Sun. Dir. Daniel Petrie. Columbia Pictures, 1961. Home video.

Sidet: Forced Exile. Dir. Salem Mekuria. Channel Four and Westdeutscher Rundfund Koln, 1991. Distributor, Women Make Movies, 1991.

So Far From India, Dir. Mira Nair. Filmakers Library, 1982. Distributor, Filmakers Library, 1982.

Star Wars. Dir. George Lucas. Fox, 1977. Home video.

Summer Nights with Greek Profile, Almond Eyes and Scent of Basil. Dir. Lina Wertmuller. Medusa, 1986. Home video.

Suzanne, Suzanne. Dir. James V. Hatch and Camille Billops. 1982. Distributor, Third World Newsreel, 1982.

Swept Away to an Unusual Destiny in the Blue Sea of August. Dir. Lina Wertmuller. Medusa, 1975. Home video.

Thelma & Louise. Dir. Ridley Scott. Pathe Entertainment, 1991. Home video.

"Twin Peaks." Exec. Prod. Mark Frost and David Lynch. Lynch/Frost Productions, 1990. Television miniseries. 7 videocassettes. Home video.

Vamp: The First Kiss Could Be Your Last. Dir. Richard Wenk. New World Pictures, 1986. Home video.

War of the Roses. Dir. Danny DeVito. Twentieth Century Fox, 1989. Home video.

Women in War: Voices from the Front Lines. Distributor, Filmakers Library, 1991.

VIDEO DISTRIBUTORS

Annenberg/CPB Collection
P.O. Box 2345
South Burlington, VT 05407–2345

Filmakers Library
124 E. 40th Street
New York, NY 10016

Films for the Humanities and Sciences
P.O. Box 2053
Princeton, NJ 08543–2053

Media Education Foundation
26 Center Street
Northampton, MA 01060

Peter Wiesner Associates
554 Taylor Avenue
Newtown, PA 28940

Pyramid Film and Video
2801 Colorado Avenue
Santa Monica, CA 90404

Third World Newsreel
335 W. 38th Street, 5th Floor
New York, NY 10018

The Voyager Company
1 Bridge Street
Irvington, NY 10533

Women Make Movies
462 Broadway, Suite 501
New York, NY 10013

Index

The Accused, 34, 107–108, 161
Ackerman, Bruce, 8
Adler, Mortimer, 4, 9–16
Adorno, Theodore, 50, 64 n.16
African, 17–18, 67–71, 75
African-American, 14–16, 18–19, 67–70, 80 nn.1–12, 133–34, 137
Agency, 23, 25
All Quiet on the Western Front, 89–91, 161
The Americanization of Emily, 87–88, 161
Andrews, Julie, 87
And Still I Rise, 68–72, 161
Angel Heart, 71, 161
Angelou, Maya, 70, 72
Army, mass, 83
Atomic bombs, 96, 98, 115, 122–24, 125 n.6, 144
Atomic Café, 122–23, 125 n.4, 161
Attenborough, Richard, 85, 162
Ayres, Lew, 90

B-52, 96
Barham, Emily (role in *The Americanization of Emily*), 87–88
Basic Instinct, 24, 161

Battle of Algiers [La Battaglia di Algeri], 86, 162
Baumer, Paul (role in *All Quiet on the Western Front*), 90–91
Bay, Edna, 75
The Beginning or the End, 123–25 n.9, 162
Bellah, Robert, 11, 21 n.13
Betts, Richard K., 96–97, 102 n.23
Billops, Camille, 72–74
Blacks. *See* African-American
Bonet, Lisa, 71
Born on the Fourth of July, 92–93, 162
Bowden, Danielle (role in *Cape Fear*), 55–59
Bowden, Leigh (role in *Cape Fear),* 55–57
Bowden, Sam (role in *Cape Fear*), 54–61
Braun, Wernher von, 98–99
Brecht, Bertolt, 116
Bunuel, Louis, 44
Burning Bed, 24, 27, 29, 162

Cady, Max (role in *Cape Fear*), 54–61

Cagney, James, 87
Cape Fear, 44, 54, 56, 59, 61–62, 162
Carby, Hazel, 69
Chartier, Roger, 32
Chayevsky, Paddy, 87
Un Chien Andalou [Andalousian Dog], 44–45, 64, 106, 162
Churchill, Winston, 87
Cinema. *See* Film
City Pages, 50
Clausewitz, Karl von, 85, 100 n.7
Clifford, Clark, 94
Close, Glenn, 27
Coburn, James, 88
Coker, George, 95
Cold War, 97–98, 105, 115, 123, 138. *See also* War
Combat, 97, 105, 115. *See also* War
Coming-of-age, 83, 91. *See also* Rite of passage
Communitarian, 7, 9–20, 83, 110–111, 134–35
Community. *See* Communitarian
Cooper, Dale (role in Twin Peaks), 50–51, 54
Cronauer, Adrian, 92
Crowther, Bosley, 99–100, 102 n.27
Cruise, Tom, 93
Culture, 12, 15, 27, 34–35, 45, 50–53, 72, 76, 81 n.15, 94–95, 102 n.29, 106, 111, 123, 132; political, 40, 83, 96; popular, 23, 27, 30, 42, 108–109; of terror, 41, 62–63
Cummings, "Bus" (role in *The Americanization of Emily*), 88

Darth Vader (role in *Star Wars*)
Dash, Julie, 35
Daughters of the Dust, 35, 162
Davis, Geena, 29, 34
Davis, Peter, 93
Dawn (War and Peace in the Nuclear Age series*), 122, 125 n.4, 162*
The Day After Trinity, 122, 124–25 n.4, 162

De Beauvoir, Simone 29
De Niro, Robert, 54
Desert Storm, Operation, 41
Deterrence, 97–98
Diawara, Manthia, 74–75
Do the Right Thing, 3–4, 13, 18–19, 162
Dr. Strangelove; Or, How I Learned to Stop Worrying and Love the Bomb, 97, 99–100, 102 nn.26–28, 162
Domination, 23–26, 33, 35, 40–43, 56, 135; sexual, 39, 41, 44, 47–48, 108
Domino thesis, 93–94
Douglas, Melvin, 87
Douglas, Michael, 27, 29
Dreamworlds, 107, 112 n.1, 162
Dunne, Frank (role in *Gallipoli*), 90

Eisenhower, Dwight D., 97
Emecheta, Buchi, 71–72
Emerson, David, 95
Emerson, Mary, 95
Enola Gay, 123–25 n.7, 162
Evil Empire, 51, 62

Faith Even to the Fire: Nuns for Social Justice, 35, 162
Fat Man and Little Boy, 124–25 n.8, 162
Fatal Attraction, 24, 27, 29, 162
Fawcett, Farah, 27, 29
Feminism, 24–25, 30, 41, 55, 107, 110, 158; criticism, 26, 52, 63–65 nn.5, 22, 25; film themes, 81 nn.13, 22; theory, 36 n.1, 43, 50
Film, depiction of women, 24–25; goals, use of, 3, 20, 55; metaphor of, 46–47; techniques for classroom showing, 32, 113, 122; theory, 42; war, 83–85
Filmmakers, 72, 77, 79, 113, 153, 158
Floyd, Randy, 95
Fonda, Henry, 12

The Force, 42
Foster, Jodie, 33
Frost, Mark, 50, 52
Fulbright, J. William, 94

Gabriel, Teshime, 75
Gallipoli, 89–91, 101 n.15, 162
Gallipoli campaign, 89–90
Galtung, Johan, 4–13, 20–21 nn.2–7
Gandhi, 85, 162
Gandhi, Mahatma, 85–86
Garner, James, 87–88
Garson, Greer, 87
Gaze, concept of, 42, 50, 52–53, 55,
    57–58
Gelb, Leslie, 96–97, 102 n.23
Gender, 18–19, 80 n.4; film represen-
    tation of, 25, 32, 36, 46–47, 51–53,
    70, 75, 79; myth, 26–27; as a vari-
    able explaining political behavior,
    30, 63–64 nn.2–4, 9–22, 40–43,
    108
Gennarino (role in *Swept Away*), 47
George, Peter, 97, 99
Gianini, Giancarlo, 47
Gibson, Mel, 91
Gitlin, Todd, 50
"Good life, the," 3–4, 6–12, 16
Good Morning, Vietnam, 92, 162
"Good war," 85–88, 101 n.9. *See also*
    "Just war"
Goods, bodily, 6–10; of character,
    10–14; economic, 10–14; mental,
    6–10; political, 10–14; social,
    10–14
The Grapes of Wrath, 3–4, 12, 19,
    162
*Greenham Challenge: Bringing Mis-
    siles to Trial,* 35, 162
Grenell, Joyce, 88

Haglin, Nancy J., 75
Hamilton, Archy (role in *Gallipoli*),
    90
Hansberry, Lorraine, 4

Hashfield, Emmett, 106
Hayden, Sterling, 98–99, 139
Hearts and Minds, 93–96, 163
Heaven and Earth, 28, 163
Hine, Darlene Clark, 70
Hollywood, 33, 83–84, 86, 120,
    123–24
hooks, bell, 69
Horkheimer, Max, 50, 64 n.16
Horton, Willie, 51
Huie, William Bradford, 87
Hurely, Nadine (role in *Twin Peaks*),
    52

Icons, 55, 69, 71, 74

Jeffords, Susan, 41
Jessup, William (role in *The Ameri-
    canization of Emily*), 87
Jhally, Sut, 107–108
Johnson, Dirk, 20 n.17
Johnson, Leo (role in *Twin Peaks*), 51
Johnson, Lyndon B., 93–94
Johnson, Michael P., 73, 80 n.9
Johnson-Odim, Cheryl, 78, 81 n.22
Jones, Grace, 71
"Just war" 83, 100 n.2, 111–12. *See
    also* "Good war"

Kahn, Herman, 98–99
Kaplan, Jonathan, 33
Keegan, John, 90
Kennan, George F., 88
Kennedy, John F., 94
Kingsley, Ben, 85
King Kong (role in *Dr. Strangelove*),
    99
Korean War, 90
Kovic, Ron, 97
Kubrick, Stanley, 97–99
Kumekucha: From Sun Up, 68, 72,
    75–77, 163

Ladd, Florence, 77, 81 n.19
Lange, Jessica, 55

Lasch, Christopher, 18–20, 21 n.15
Lee, Mark, 91
Lee, Spike, 4, 13–14
LeMay, Curtis, 98
Levée en masse, 85
Lewis, Juliette, 55
Liberals, 4, 7–8, 11, 15–17, 20,
    133–34
Locke, John, 10, 11
Loyalty, 9, 11, 18, 20
Lynch, David, 50–51

Maddy (role in *Twin Peaks*), 53, 106
Madison, Charles E. (role in *The
    Americanization of Emily*), 87–88
Maids and Madams, 35, 163
Mandrake, Lionel (role in *Dr.
    Strangelove*), 99
Manhattan Project, 120, 123–25
Marshall, William, 96
Martell, Catherine (role in *Twin
    Peaks)*, 52
Martin, Jean, 86
Marton, Lori, 55
Masculinity, 28, 41. *See also*
    Coming-of-age; Rite of passage
Massive retaliation doctrine, 97–98
McNamara, Robert S., 94
Mekuria, Salem, 77–79
Melato, Mariangela, 46–47
Mercer, Kobena, 69
Milestone, Lewis, 89
Milken, Michael (role in *Twin Peaks*),
    51
Miller, Henry, 55
Millett, Kate, 47, 58
Milne, Tom, 100, 102 n.28
Mississippi Burning, 24, 163
Mitchem, Robert, 54
M'mbugu-Schelling, Helen, 72,
    75–77
Mobilization, mass, 85, 86
Mookie (role in *Do the Right Thing*),
    14–15
Morgan, David, 28

Motion picture. *See* Film
Movie. *See* Film
Mrs. Miniver, 87–88, 163
Muffley, Merkin (role in *Dr. Strange-
    love*), 99
Muller, Robert, 95
Mulvey, Laura, 42, 63 n.5, 158

The Nasty Girl, 35, 163
Nation, 50
National Review, 51
Nationalism, 85
Nichols, Bill, 77
Niebuhr, Reinhold, 18–19, 21 n.16
Nolte, Nick, 54

Official Story [La historia oficial],
    34, 163
Okies, 11, 13, 17–19, 134
Onwurah, Ngozi, 68, 70–72, 161
Oppenheimer, J. Robert, 123
Osborn, George K., 97

Paglia, Camille, 30
Palmer, Bob (role in *Twin Peaks*),
    53–54
Palmer, Laura (role in *Twin Peaks*),
    50–53, 64 n.17, 106
Palmer, Leland (role in *Twin Peaks*),
    53–54
Patriotism, 85, 91–92
Peace, 10, 18, 21 n.7, 25–27; antiwar
    activism, 41, 80 n.1; conceptual-
    ized, 3–5, 7–8, 12–13, 15, 20 n.2
Peace movement, 89, 101 n.13, 125
    n.3
Peck, Gregory, 54
Perry, William, 118–19
Piaget, Jean, 118
Pickens, "Slim," 99
Pidgeon, Walter, 87
Placido, Michele, 47
Platoon, 92, 163
Pretty Woman, 24, 163
Protector, 28–29

Pulaski, Ronette (role in *Twin Peaks*), 50

Race, 47, 70, 79, 83 n.4, 108, 111, 133, 136, 145
Raffaella (role in *Swept Away*), 46–47
Raheem, Radio (role in *Do the Right Thing*), 15–16, 133–34
A Raisin in the Sun, 3–4, 16, 18–19, 163
Rape: act of, 33, 43, 47, 53, 55, 59, 70, 106–108, 110–111; cultural predisposition toward, 28, 34–35, 39, 51, 55, 68; metaphor, as, 39, 41, 47; terror of, 28, 31, 36 n.1, 70–72
Ravenal, Earl C., 96, 102 n.24
Reagan, Ronald, 51, 64 nn.15, 22, 159
Remarque, Erich Maria, 89
Resistance, 19–20, 23, 25, 29–30, 32–33, 37 n.2, 71
Revolution: American, 85; French, 85
Ripper, Jack D. (Role in *Dr. Strangelove*), 98–99
Rite of passage, 85, 90–92. *See also* Coming-of-age
Roiphe, Katie, 30, 36 n.1
Rolling Stone, 52, 64 n.24
Roosevelt, Franklin D., 86, 89
Rosenfield, Albert (role in *Twin Peaks*), 54
Rousseau, Jean Jacques, 100
Royce, Josiah, 18

Sal (role in *Do The Right Thing*), 14–16, 133
Sandel, Michael, 9, 21 n.9
Sarandon, Susan, 29, 34
Schneider, Bert, 93
Scorsese, Martin, 54–55, 61, 162
Scott, George C., 99
Scott, James C., 33, 34, 37 n.18
Scott, Ridley, 34, 163
Sellers, Peter, 99

Sherwin, Martin, 123
Sidet, 68, 77–78, 81 n.19, 163
Sidet: Forced Exile, 68, 77–78, 81 n.19, 163
Simpson, Nicole Brown, 24
Skywalker, Luke (role in *Star Wars*), 42
Slavery, 67–69
Smedlap, Professor (role in David Pace essay), 113, 115–17
Smith, Valerie, 74
Soglin, Paul, 20
Soldier, 84–85, 90–92, 100–101 nn.3, 8, 13, 17–19
Soper, Kate, 30, 37 n.9
Sowders, Edward, 95
Star Wars, 42, 51, 163
Steinbeck, John, 4, 13
Stereotype, 23–24, 26–27, 36 n.2, 52, 69, 70, 80 n.4
Stiehm, Judith Hicks, 28
Stone, Oliver, 28, 92, 162–63
Stouffer, Samuel, 92
Strangelove, Doctor (role in *Dr. Strangelove*), 99
Strategic Air Command (SAC), 96, 98–99
Structural violence. *See* Violence
Summer Nights with Greek Profile, Almond Eyes and Scent of Basil, 44, 46–47, 49, 163
Surrealism, 44–45, 49–53, 64 nn.8, 11, 107, 136
Survival, strategy of, 68, 77–79
Suzanne, Suzanne, 68, 72–73, 75, 163
Swept Away to an Unusual Destiny in the Blue Sea of August, 44, 46–47, 49, 163

Taylor, Stephen, 99
Teller, Edward J., 99
Terrorism, 39–40, 43–44, 62, 73, 80, 102 n.29, 106
Terrorist, 48, 86
Terry, Avril "Honey," 106

Thelma & Louise, 24, 29, 34, 163
Theweleit, Klaus, 41, 63 n.4
Transcendence, 29
Transcripts, hidden, 33
Truman, Harry S. (President), 97, 123
Truman, Harry S. (role in *Twin Peaks*), 50–51, 53–54
Turgidson, "Buck" (role in *Dr. Strangelove*), 99
"Twin Peaks," 44, 49–53, 61–62, 64 nn.8, 15, 19, 22–23, 106–107, 163

Vamp: The First Kiss Could Be Your Last, 71, 163
Verhoeven, Michael, 35, 161, 163
Vietnam, 28, 41, 63, 90–96, 100–102 nn.7, 19–20, 22–23, 25, 138, 143–46, 156–59, 162. *See also* War
Violence: defined, 3, 4, 5; domestic, 31, 67–68, 70, 72–73, 80 n.10; legitimate, 25, 27–28, 40, 43, 63; non-violence, 23, 26, 28–29, 86; physical, 4, 13–15, 19, 68; political, 39–44, 46–47, 61–64 n.8; sexual, 39–47, 49, 52–55, 57, 59–64 n.8; structural, 3, 4, 6, 8, 10–14, 19–21 n.10, 67–69, 73, 79–80 n.1

Walker, Juliet E. K., 67–68, 80 n.1, 137
War, casualties, 31, 37 n.14; defined, 100 n.1; democratization of, 85; distinctive features of as a form of social contract, 83; experience of, 40–41, 67–68, 84–100
War of the Roses, 100 n.1, 163
Warrior, 40, 91
Wayne, John, 28
Weir, Peter, 91
Wertmuller, Lina, 44, 46–49, 163
Westmoreland, William, 94–95
Williams, Linda, 46, 64 nn.11–12
Williams, Robin, 92
Women in War: Voices from the Front Lines, 35, 163
Woolf, Virginia, 26
World War I, 88, 90
World War II, 84, 87–88, 92, 96, 98
Wright, Teresa, 87
Wynn, Keenan, 88

Younger family (roles in *Raisin in the Sun*), 16–18; Beneatha, 16–17; Mama, 16–17; Ruth, 16–17; Travis, 16; Walter, 16–17

About the Contributors

BARBARA ALLEN is Associate Professor of Political Science at Carleton College, Northfield, MN. She holds B.A., M.A., and Ph.D. degrees from Indiana University. Professor Allen's scholarly interests focus on the democratic ideas of Alexis de Tocqueville and the life and thought of Dr. Martin Luther King, Jr. She is a contributing editor for the Martin Luther King Papers Project at Stanford University and has given a number of papers on both men's and women's work. She is also coauthor of a study of public opinion during the Gulf War; author of two articles on women, violence, and the media; and author of a number of articles and presentations on various pedagogical issues. Her professional activities include service on the Film and Politics subsection of the American Political Science Association.

KRISTINE R. BRANCOLINI has been Head of Media and Reserve Services, and Librarian for Film Studies at Indiana University since 1983. She also teaches a course in media librarianship in the School of Library and Information Science. She holds a B.A. in English from Scripps College and an M.L.S. from Indiana University. She completed her coursework for a Ph.D. in instructional systems technology at Indiana University. Recent publications include *Video Collections and Multimedia in ARL Libraries: Making Tomorrow's Decisions Today*, with Rick E. Provine (In press); *Video Collections and Multimedia in ARL Libraries: Changing Technologies* (Occasional Paper #19), with Rick E. Provine (1997); "Video Collections in Academic Libraries," in *Video Collection Development in Multi-Type Libraries: A Handbook*, edited by Gary P. Handman (Greenwood Press,

1994); "Film Studies Collections," with Beverly Teach, in *Managing Performing Arts Collections in Academic and Public Libraries*, edited by Carolyn A. Sheehy (Greenwood Press, 1994); and "Patterns of Video and Film Use at Indiana University," with Beverly Teach; *College & University Media Review* (Summer 1994).

GLORIA J. GIBSON is Associate Professor of Afro-American Studies at Indiana University. She is also the Director of the Archives of Traditional Music, Assistant Director of the Black Film Center/Archive, and the recipient of a 1992–93 Ford Foundation Postdoctoral Fellowship. Her publications can be found in books such as *Multiple Voices in Feminist Film Criticism* and in journals such as *Wide Angle*, *Quarterly Review of Film & Television*, and *Western Journal of Black Studies*. She is completing a book-length manuscript entitled "Moving Tableaux of Consciousness: The Films and Videos of Black Women of the African Diaspora."

JOHN P. LOVELL was the first (1989–94) Director of the multidisciplinary Indiana Center on Global Change and World Peace and is Professor Emeritus of Political Science, Indiana University, Bloomington. His interest in the process by which governments and societies learn—or fail to learn—from the experience of war is illustrated in his article in the October 1992 issue of *Peace and Change*, " 'Lessons Learned': From Vietnam to the Gulf War." A related interest in the distinctive cultures of organizations, such as the American armed forces, that are entrusted with the "management of violence" in defense of society and its vital interests is reflected in his book, *Neither Athens nor Sparta? The American Service Academies in Transition* (1979). His current research and teaching is focused on a broader policy concern, the challenge that democracies face of reconciling demands made in the name of national security with democratic values.

WILLIAM J. MEYER is Assistant Professor of Ethics, Religion and Philosophy at Maryville College, Maryville, TN. He has a Ph.D. in Ethics and Society from the University of Chicago. His research and teaching interests focus on religion, ethics, and politics. He served as the Center Associate for Programs at the Indiana Center on Global Change and World Peace from 1990 to 1993 and as a Research Associate at Indiana University's Poynter Center for the Study of Ethics and American Institutions, 1989 to 1993.

DAVID PACE is Associate Professor of History, Indiana University, Bloomington. He teaches courses (supplemented by film) on War and Society in the 20th Century, on The Dawn of the Atomic Age, and on Struggle, Conflict, and Competition in Modern European Thought. Ongoing research interests are reflected in his article "The Battle Over the Next War: Ideology, Politics, and the Image of Nuclear War in Post-Hiroshima France," in *The Image of War in Literature, Media, and Society*, edited by W. Wright and S. Kaplan (1992); and he is working on a monograph on French reactions to the nuclear issues of the 1940s. Also has a keen interest in the pedagogical concerns of teaching, Pace has written and lectured on various techniques found to be effective in developing cognitive skills.

JEAN C. ROBINSON is Associate Professor in Political Science, East Asian Studies and Women's Studies at Indiana University, Bloomington. She received her Ph.D. from Cornell University and has done research in Asia and Eastern Europe. Her primary specialty is the People's Republic of China, although she has researched and published on gender and work issues in Japan, Poland, France, and Korea as well as China. She has published and consulted widely, including serving on the advisory panel to the United Nations Commission on Science and Technology to devise appropriate programs for Women in Science and Technology in Developing Countries. Currently she is writing a manuscript on gender, family, and work in China and Poland. Her major research interests focus on the ways in which women find a will and a voice to resist, whether it be resisting the domination of states or the domination of male power. She currently teaches comparative courses in both Political Science and in Women's Studies and is completing a textbook for use in Introductory Comparative Politics classes.

ISBN 0-275-95972-4

90000>

EAN

9 780275 959722

HARDCOVER BAR CODE